The OXFORD Children's A to Z of

World Religions

Anita Ganeri

OXFORD
UNIVERSITY PRESS

Oxford University Press, Great Clarendon Street, Oxford OX2 6DP

Oxford New York

Athens Auckland Bangkok Bogotá Buenos Aires
Calcutta Cape Town Chennai Dar es Salaam
Delhi Florence Hong Kong Istanbul Karachi
Kuala Lumpur Madrid Melbourne Mexico City
Mumbai Nairobi Paris São Paulo Singapore
Taipei Tokyo Toronto Warsaw
and associated companies in
Berlin Ibadan

Oxford is a registered trade mark of
Oxford University Press

Text copyright © Anita Ganeri 1999

British Library Cataloguing in Publication Data
Data available

First published 1999

ISBN 0–19–910468–9 (paperback)
ISBN 0–19–910467–0 (hardback)

10 9 8 7 6 5 4 3 2 1

Printed in Italy

Acknowledgements

Design: White Design

Picture research: Caroline Wood

Religious consultants: Penny Faust,
Basil Mustapha, Ruth Nason

Abbreviations: t = top; b = bottom; l = left;
r = right; c = centre; back = background

Photographs

The publishers would like to thank the following
for permission to reproduce the following
photographs:

By permission of the British Library: 34

© Copyright The British Museum: cover tl, 7, 16c

Corbis: Gianni Dagli Orti, 4, 22b; Robert Holmes, 5t, 12b; The
National Gallery, London, 5c, 34-35; Bojan Brecelj, 6t; Dave
Bartruff, 6b, 42; Philip Gould, 81; David Reed, 8-9; Charles &
Josette Lenars, 10; Eye Ubiquitous, 11t, 12tr, 24-25; 56b, 57b;
Dean Conger, 13; Ted Spiegel, 14t; Nik Wheeler, 14b; David
Muench, 17t; Owen Franken, 17b; Douglas Peebles, 18t; Sheld
Collins, 20, 41t; Leonard de Selva, cover bl, br, 22t; Michael S.
Yamashita, 26-27, 55t, 64c; Arvind Garg, 25, 45; Ric Ergenbri
28tr; Philadelphia Museum of Art, 28b, 46b; David S. Robbins
29; Craig Lovell, 33t; Paul Almasy, 33b; Richard T. Nowitz, 36
48, 52, 61t, 63, 64tl; Keren Su, 39; David Lees, 40; The State
Russian Museum, 41b; Michael Nicholson, 43; Chris Hellier, 4
Sakamoto Photo Research Laboratory, 47; Vittoriano Rastelli,
49t, 62-63, Jeremy Horner, 49b; Angelo Hornak, 50-51; Brian
Vikander, 53t; Jacqui Hurst, 53b; Christine Osborne, 57t; Aliso
Wright, 58; David H. Wells, 59; Royal Ontario Museum,
60; Nazima Kowall, 61b

Corel: 16t, 28tc, 32t, 56t

E.T. Archive: Bibliothèque Nationale, Paris, 18b

Glasgow Museums: The St Mungo Museum of Religious Life
and Art; 15t

Michael Holford: Musée Guimet, Paris, 11b

Copyright Imperial War Museum, London: 30t

The Jewish Museum, London: 37b

Magnum Photos: © Abbas, 21b, 31, 32b, 38/© Fred Mayer, 37t;
© Raghu Rai, 46t

Panos Pictures: © Liba Taylor, 15b

© Ann & Bury Peerless – Picture Library: 25b

Photodisc: 12c, 36tc

Trip: Dinodia, 21t; H. Rogers, 30bl

Illustrations and diagrams

Gerry Ball 19, 23, 54, 60

Clive Goodyer 5, 9, 11, 31

John Haslam 20, 46

Sheila Moxley 4, 13, 24, 40

Andrea Norton 35, 45, 50, 59

Helen Parsley 7, 36, 51, 56

Martin Sanders 14, 16, 29, 32, 36, 39, 43, 62

Yehuda Sinai 27,

Dear Reader

Have you ever wondered how the world was created, why you are here, or what will happen when you die? Do you believe in God? If you do, what is he like and where can you find him? These are difficult questions for anyone to answer. But this is what the world's religions try to do.

What is a religion? A religion is a set of beliefs and a way of worship. In most religions, people worship a great power which gives special meaning to their lives. Some people call this power God. Others follow the teachings of religious teachers, using them as a guide for their lives. For many people, their own religion, or faith, is the most important thing in their lives. It helps them to find the right way to live and to share their joys and sorrows.

The six main religions in the world today are **Buddhism, Christianity, Hinduism, Islam, Judaism** and **Sikhism**. You can find them all in this book, and lots more besides. Learn about religious places and people. Find out how festivals are celebrated around the world. And, whether you are religious or not, enjoy discovering the different ways of believing which go into making up our world.

Anita Ganeri

Abraham

In **Christianity**, **Islam** and **Judaism**, Abraham is a **prophet** who lived about 4,000 years ago in the Middle East. In Islam, he is known by the **Arabic** form of his name: Ibrahim. The **scriptures** of all three religions tell how Abraham taught people that there is only one true **God** and that they should **worship** only Him.

In Judaism, Abraham (Avraham in **Hebrew**) is called the father of the **Jewish** people. See also **Allah**, **Id ul-Adha**, **Ka'aba**, **patriarch**.

AD

AD stands for the Latin words Anno Domini, meaning 'in the year of the Lord'. AD is used in dates: for example, AD 2000, which means the 2000th year after the time (taken as year 0) when **Jesus** was born. The use of AD comes from **Christian beliefs**. Often **CE** is used instead.
See also **BC**, **BCE**, **calendar**.

△
Abraham was ready to obey God, even when he believed God wanted him to sacrifice his son. God gave him a ram to sacrifice instead.

▽
Some Christians light an Advent candle on each day of the period leading up to Christmas.

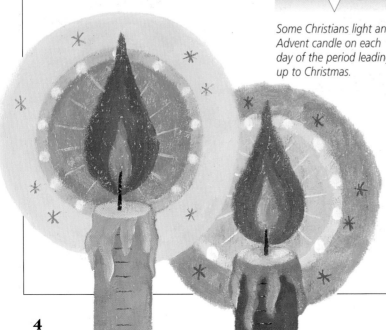

adhan

In **Islam**, the adhan is the call to **prayer** (**salah**), announcing the start of each of the five daily prayer times. In **Islamic** countries, the call is made from **mosques**, sometimes by a **muezzin** and sometimes by a recorded voice over a loudspeaker.

Many **Muslim** parents whisper the adhan into the right ear of their new-born baby, so that the call to prayer is the first thing that the child hears.

Adi Granth

The Adi Granth (meaning 'first book') is one name for the **Sikh** **scriptures**, which were put together by **Guru** Arjan Dev, the fifth Sikh Guru. Later, **Guru Gobind Singh**, the tenth Sikh Guru, told Sikhs to call their scriptures the **Guru Granth Sahib**. See also **Sikhism**.

Advent

For **Christians**, Advent is the period including four Sundays before **Christmas**. Advent means 'coming' and during this time Christians prepare for the Christmas celebration of the birth, or coming into the world, of **Jesus**.

afterlife

The afterlife is an idea that helps to explain what happens to people when they die. The idea is that each person has a **soul**, which continues to live after the person's death. In some religions, including **Hinduism** and **Sikhism**, the belief is that, after a person's death, the soul is reborn in another body. See also **Day of Judgement**, **heaven**, **hell**, **paradise**, **reincarnation**, **resurrection**.

agnostic

An agnostic is someone who says that it is impossible to know for certain if **God** exists or not because there is no proof.

ahimsa

Ahimsa means not hurting or killing any living creature. It is an important idea in **Buddhism**, **Hinduism** and **Jainism**.

Part of practising ahimsa for followers of Jainism is to wear a mask, to stop them breathing in and killing insects.

Allah

Allah is the **Islamic** name for **God**. It is an **Arabic** word meaning 'the God'.
See also **Islam**.

altar

In a **Christian church**, the altar is the table used for the **Eucharist**.

amen

Christians, **Jews** and **Muslims** say 'Amen' at the end of **prayers**. It means 'it is true'.

amrit

Amrit is a special mixture of sugar and water used at **Sikh** **ceremonies**.
See also **Khalsa**.

Amritsar

Amritsar is a city in north-west India. It was founded in the late 16th century by **Guru** Ram Das (see **Sikhism**) and became a religious and trading centre for **Sikhs**. The most important building in Amritsar is the **Golden Temple**.

'Angel in Green', painted by Leonardo da Vinci, 1483.

angel

In **Christianity**, **Islam** and **Judaism**, angels are heavenly beings who carry messages between **God** and people on earth. One angel named in the **scriptures** of the three religions is **Gabriel**.

Anglican

The Anglican **Church** is one branch of a group of **Christians** called **Protestants**. In England, the Anglican Church is called the Church of England. In the USA, it is called the Episcopal Church.

apostle

For **Christians**, an apostle is someone sent out to spread the message of **Jesus**. The first apostles were **Jesus's** **disciples**. Later, they were joined by Paul, who had become a Christian after seeing a vision of Jesus. 'The Acts of the Apostles' is a book in the **Bible** which tells of the growth of the early **Church** and of Paul's **missionary** journeys.

aqiqah

Aqiqah is a **ceremony** that is often held when a **Muslim** baby is seven days old. After the baby has been named, its head is shaved and the hair is weighed. The value of the same weight of silver is calculated, and the **family** gives that value in money to the poor. **Prayers** are said for the baby's future.

Arabic

Arabic is the language in which the **Qur'an**, the **Islamic** holy book, is written. **Muslims** believe that the words of the Qur'an came from **Allah** and were first spoken by the **Prophet Muhammad** in Arabic. They believe that the words of the Qur'an should never be changed. Muslims everywhere learn to recite verses from the Qur'an, and say their **prayers** in Arabic.
See also **madrasah**.

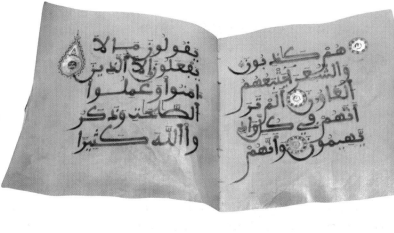

△

For Muslims, the Arabic of the Qur'an is the most beautiful example of the language to listen to. Artists and calligraphers make beautiful copies of the book, like this one from the 14th century.

ardas

The ardas is a **prayer** said at most **Sikh services**. It remembers **God**, the teachings of the Sikh **Gurus**, and people who died for **Sikhism**. It also asks God to **bless** all Sikhs and everyone else in the world. The names of particular people may be included in the ardas.

ark

• In the **Christian** and **Jewish scriptures**, the ark is a boat that **God** told **Noah** to build to save his family and two of every animal and bird from a great flood.

• In the **Christian** and **Jewish scriptures**, the Ark of the **Covenant** is a wooden chest covered in gold. It was made by the **Jews** in the time of **Moses**, to hold the stone tablets on which the **Ten Commandments** or **Ten Sayings** were inscribed.

• In a **synagogue**, the ark is a cupboard in which the **Torah** scrolls are kept. Named after the Ark of the Covenant, it is usually on the wall that faces towards **Jerusalem**.
See also **Judaism**.

 The Ten Sayings are written above this ark in a synagogue in Jerusalem.

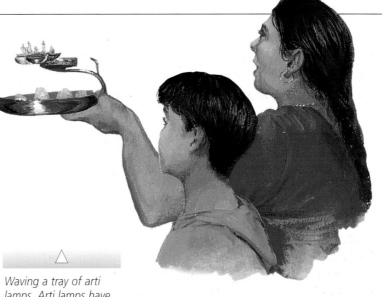

arti

Arti is part of **Hindu worship**. A tray of five arti lamps is waved in a circular movement in front of a **murti** (image of a **god** or **goddess**). Then worshippers hold their hands over the lamps and touch their faces to feel the warmth of the god's or goddess's **blessing**.

Ascension

The Ascension ('going up') of **Jesus** is celebrated by **Christians** forty days after **Easter**. According to the Christian **scriptures**, Jesus remained on earth for forty days after he had risen from the dead. Then he was lifted up into **heaven**, to be with **God**. See also **Christianity**.

Waving a tray of arti lamps. Arti lamps have a wick or wicks soaked in oil or ghee (clarified butter).

Ash Wednesday

Ash Wednesday is the first day of **Lent**, a period in the **Christian** year. At some **church services**, people are 'ashed': a cross is marked on their forehead with a paste of ashes – a sign of repentance (being sorry for one's sins).

This figure of Avalokiteshvara was made in India about one thousand years ago.

ashrama

In **Hindu belief** an ashrama is a stage in life. There are four ashramas, each with its own duties. In the first 'student' stage Hindus learn about **Hinduism**. In the second 'householder' stage they work for their living, get married and have a family. The third stage is retirement. Long ago, people left their families at this time and went to the forest to pray and **meditate**. Today, most people stay at home. The fourth stage is to become a wandering holy man. Most Hindus do not follow this stage.

atheist

An atheist is someone who does not believe that **God** exists.

atman

See **Hinduism**.

aum

Aum (sometimes spelled 'om') is a sound that **Hindus chant** at the beginning and end of **prayers** and **hymns**. The sound represents the sound of Brahman (see **Hinduism**). The written form of 'aum' is an important Hindu **symbol**.

Avalokiteshvara

Avalokiteshvara is a **bodhisattva**. As a sign of being ready to help anyone, Avalokiteshvara is often shown with a thousand arms, each with an eye and holding an object. See also **Dalai Lama**.

avatar

In **Hindu belief** an avatar is the body or shape a **god** or **goddess** takes to visit the earth.

ayatollah

An ayatollah is a **Muslim** who has studied **Islamic** theology and law to a very high degree. The leader of the **Shi'a** Muslims is an ayatollah.

B

Baha'i

The Baha'i religion began in Persia (now Iran) in the 19th century. Its first preachers were a holy man called the Bab and his follower, Baha'u'llah.
They taught that all people and all religions are equal. Today, there are about 3.5 million Baha'is all over the world.

Many people have come to be baptised in the river at this 'Believers' Baptism' in Haiti.

baptism

Baptism is a **ceremony** that takes place in many **Christian churches**. It involves sprinkling or pouring **water** on the person being baptized, or dipping the person in water, as a **symbol** of washing away his or her 'old life' without **Jesus**.

Some churches baptize babies. At the ceremony, the baby's parents promise to bring up their child to believe in and follow Jesus.

Other churches have a ceremony called 'Believers' Baptism', for adults who have made up their own minds to follow Jesus.
See also **Christianity**, **John the Baptist**.

Bar Mitzvah

The name Bar Mitzvah ('son of the commandment') is given to a **Jewish** boy when he is 13 years old and starts his adult life. He must then obey all the Jewish laws. At his Bar Mitzvah **ceremony** in the **synagogue**, the boy recites a **prayer** and reads from the **Torah**. Then he is **blessed** and may be reminded of his new duties. Afterwards there is a meal to celebrate this happy day.
See also **Judaism**, **Ten Sayings**.

Baisakhi

Baisakhi is an Indian new year **festival** celebrated by **Sikhs**. On the international **calendar** the festival takes place in April. A tradition at Baisakhi is to take down the **Nishan Sahib**, the flag outside all **gurdwaras**, clean the flagpole, and hoist a new flag. It was at Baisakhi in 1699 that **Guru Gobind Singh** founded the **Khalsa**, the Sikh community. Today many Sikhs choose the time of Baisakhi for the **amrit ceremony** by which they join the Khalsa.

Bat Hayil

In **Orthodox Jewish** communities, Bat Hayil ('daughter of valour') is a name sometimes given to girls when they start their adult lives. Jewish girls are considered adult at age 12.

Bat Mitzvah

For **Progressive Jews**, Bat Mitzvah ('daughter of the commandment') is the girls' equivalent of **Bar Mitzvah**. A girl becomes Bat Mitzvah when she is 12.

BC

BC stands for Before **Christ**. It is used in dates: for example, 75 BC, which means the 75th year before the time (taken as year 0) when **Jesus** (Christ) was born. Often **BCE** is used instead of BC.
See also **AD**, **calendar**, **CE**.

BCE

BCE stands for Before the Common Era. It is often used instead of **BC**, which is suitable for **Christians** but not for people of other religions. See also **AD**, **calendar**, **CE**.

belief

Having a belief in something means thinking or accepting that it is true. For example, belief in **God** means accepting that God exists. See also **creed**.

bell

Bells are used in several ways in religious **services**. For example, when they go into a **temple**, **Hindus** and **Jains** ring a large bell. Its sound clears their minds ready for **worship**. Some **Christian churches** have bells that are rung before services, and in some churches bells are rung to mark each part of a service.

At his Bar Mitzvah ceremony in the synagogue, a Jewish boy reads aloud from the Torah. He uses a yad (pointer) to keep his place.

Bethlehem

Bethlehem is a town in **Israel** where **Jesus** was born. The **Christian scriptures** tell how Jesus's parents, **Mary** and **Joseph**, travelled to Bethlehem to take part in a census. The only place they could find to stay was a stable behind an inn, and it was here that Jesus was born. Today, the **Church** of the **Nativity** in Bethlehem marks Jesus's birthplace.
See also **Christianity**, **Christmas**.

Bhagavad Gita

The Bhagavad Gita ('Song of the Lord') is part of the **Mahabharata** and is probably the most loved of the **Hindu scriptures**. The story tells of a quarrel and war between two royal families. Prince Arjuna is reluctant to begin fighting because the enemy army is led by his cousins. The **god Krishna** appears and reminds Arjuna that he must do his duty as a soldier, without thinking of himself.

Different cultures around the world use different kinds and shapes of bell.

bhikkhu

A bhikkhu is a **Buddhist monk**. Buddhist **nuns** are called bhikkhuni. A Buddhist may become a bhikkhu or bhikkhuni for the rest of his or her life or for a few months or years. Buddhist monks and nuns live in a **monastery** or **vihara**, and take vows to lead a simple life, with few possessions.

In different types of **Buddhism**, monks wear different-coloured robes. **Zen** monks wear black, Tibetan monks (known as **lamas**) wear maroon and **Theravada** monks wear saffron (deep yellow). Saffron was the colour worn by the first Buddhist monks, who lived in the forest. They found that the colour did not scare or upset the forest animals.
See also **Kathina**, **Sangha**.

Bible

The Bible is the name of the **Christian scriptures**. It consists of the **Old Testament**, which comes from the ancient **Jewish** scriptures, and the New Testament. The New Testament contains accounts of the life of **Jesus** and the experiences of the early Christians. See also **Tenakh**, **Torah**.

bimah

In a **synagogue**, the bimah is a table or desk from which the **Torah** scrolls are read.

birth

When a baby is born, most religions have special **ceremonies** to celebrate, give thanks and make promises about the child's future. See **aqiqah**, **baptism**, **circumcision**, **names**.

bishop

Senior **ministers** in the **Anglican**, **Roman Catholic**, **Orthodox Christian** and some other **churches** are called bishops.

Bismillah

Bismillah ('in the name of **Allah**') is the first word in an **Arabic** saying that begins every chapter ('surah') in the **Qur'an** (except the ninth). Many **Muslims** say the Bismillah before they begin any task.

bless, blessing

To bless someone means to hope for or bring on them a feeling of deep happiness that comes from **God** or the **gods**. To bless something means to say or show that it is becoming **holy** in some way.

Blessing is also the name of a short **prayer** said by **Christians** and **Jews**.

A bishop, carrying his crozier (staff), speaks to a group of young people.

Bodh Gaya

Bodh Gaya is a town in north-east India where the **Buddha** gained **enlightenment**. There is a great golden statue of the Buddha in the Mahabodhi **Temple** there, which is visited by **Buddhist pilgrims** from all over the world.

bodhi tree

The bodhi tree ('tree of **enlightenment**') in **Bodh Gaya** is a descendant of the tree under which the **Buddha meditated**.

bodhisattva

In **Mahayana Buddhism**, bodhisattvas are enlightened beings who could enter **Nirvana**. Instead, they choose to be reborn, so that they can help others gain **enlightenment** too. Mahayana Buddhists try to follow the bodhisattvas' example of kindness and unselfishness. See also **Avalokiteshvara**, **Pure Land**.

Brahma

Brahma is one of the three most important **Hindu gods**. He is the creator of the world, and the god of wisdom. Images of Brahma show him with four faces, to give the idea that he sees and knows everything. In his four arms he holds the **sacred** texts, **prayer** beads, **holy water** and a spoon used in **worship** ('puja'). See also **creation**, **Hinduism**, **Shiva**, **Vishnu**.

The Mahabodhi ('Great Enlightenment') Temple in Bodh Gaya, India.

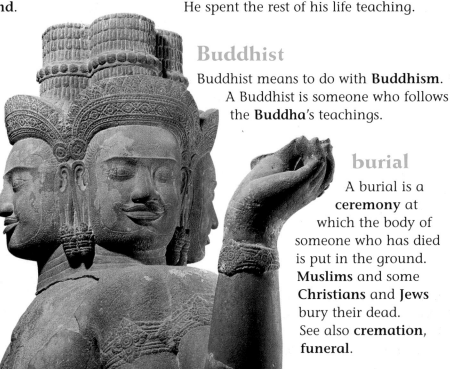

▷ *A stone image of Brahma.*

Brahman

See **Hinduism**.

Brahmin

A Brahmin is a member of the highest **Hindu caste**. Hindu **priests** come from this group.

Buddha

The Buddha ('enlightened one') is the name given by **Buddhists** to Siddhartha Gautama (c.480 - c.400 **BCE**), whose teachings they follow.

Siddhartha was an Indian prince. His father kept him away from the world outside his palace, so he would never know unhappiness. But one day, out riding, Siddhartha saw an old man, a sick man and a dead man – his first sight of suffering. Then he saw a **holy** man. He became a wandering holy man himself, seeking to understand why there is suffering and how it could be ended. After six years, he found the answers as he **meditated** at **Bodh Gaya**. He spent the rest of his life teaching.

Buddhist

Buddhist means to do with **Buddhism**. A Buddhist is someone who follows the **Buddha's** teachings.

burial

A burial is a **ceremony** at which the body of someone who has died is put in the ground. **Muslims** and some **Christians** and **Jews** bury their dead. See also **cremation**, **funeral**.

Buddhism

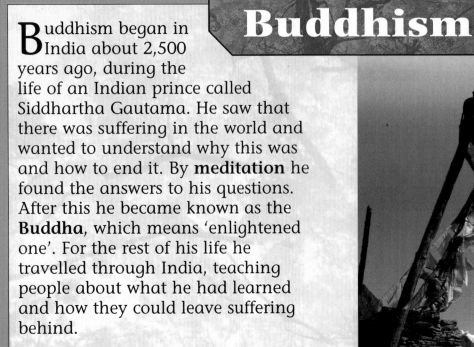

Buddhism began in India about 2,500 years ago, during the life of an Indian prince called Siddhartha Gautama. He saw that there was suffering in the world and wanted to understand why this was and how to end it. By **meditation** he found the answers to his questions. After this he became known as the **Buddha**, which means 'enlightened one'. For the rest of his life he travelled through India, teaching people about what he had learned and how they could leave suffering behind.

Buddhists are people who follow the Buddha's teachings. They do not **worship** the Buddha as a **god**, but he is a guide for their lives. Today, there are over 400 million Buddhists all over the world. Many live in Asia, in countries such as Sri Lanka, Thailand and Japan.

Types of Buddhism

There are two main types of Buddhism: **Theravada** and **Mahayana**. Mahayana includes many different branches of the religion, such as **Pure Land**, Tibetan Buddhism and **Zen**.

△
Buddhist prayer flags are a sign of loving kindness being sent into the world.

▷

Many statues of the Buddha show him touching the ground, as a sign that the Buddhist way is 'down to earth', a way of living in the real world.

Monasteries

Some followers of Buddhism choose to become **monks** or **nuns** (see **bhikkhu** and **lama**). Most of them shave their heads, wear simple robes, and give up their possessions, except for items that they really need. They live in a **monastery** or **vihara**.

The Four Noble Truths

The Buddha called suffering 'dukkha' (things that are hard to bear). This is what he taught about it:
- Life is full of dukkha.
- Dukkha happens because people are greedy and selfish and never happy with what they have.
- People can leave dukkha behind.
- The way to do this is to follow the Noble Eightfold Path.

The Noble Eightfold Path

The Noble Eightfold Path is also known as the Middle Way. It shows eight ways for people to live. The Buddha said that people should try to follow all these paths.
- Right understanding. This means understanding the Four Noble Truths.
- Right thought. This means thinking good, kind thoughts.
- Right speech. This means not telling lies or saying unkind things.
- Right action. This means behaving thoughtfully and kindly towards others.
- Right work. This means doing a job that does not harm others or the environment.
- Right effort. This means trying hard to do good things.
- Right mindfulness. This means thinking carefully before you speak or act.
- Right concentration. This means using meditation to help train your mind. This helps you to be a peaceful person.

The Eightfold Path out of suffering is represented by an eight-spoked wheel.

The Five Promises

In their daily lives, Buddhists try to keep these five promises:
- Not to kill or harm living things.
- Not to steal.
- Not to use their sexuality in a harmful way.
- Not to lie or say unkind things.
- Not to drink alcohol or take drugs.

Nirvana

Buddhists believe that by following the Buddha's teachings they can eventually leave behind all suffering and gain the state of peace and happiness known as **Nirvana**.

The Three Jewels

Buddhists call the Buddha, his teaching (the **Dharma**) and the Buddhist community everywhere (the **Sangha**) the Three Jewels or the Three Refuges. Every day, Buddhists say these words:

*'I go to the Buddha as my refuge.
I go to the Dharma as my refuge.
I go to the Sangha as my refuge.'*

A refuge is somewhere to go to feel very safe.

Honouring the Buddha

When Buddhists worship, they show their respect for the Buddha. Some Buddhists have a **shrine** at home with a small statue of the Buddha. Every day, they repeat the Three Jewels and the Five Promises and offer gifts of flowers, **candles** and incense to the Buddha. They also read from the holy books and spend some time in meditation. This type of worship is called 'puja'.

Some Buddhists visit a vihara for puja led by the monks. They take off their shoes before entering the shrine room. Then they sit or kneel in front of the statue of the Buddha and say the Three Jewels and the Five Promises after the monks.

Monks put their hands together and bow in front of the shrine.

calendar

A calendar is a system for dividing and naming time. Different **cultures** have developed different calendars. But it is also necessary to have a single calendar for everyone around the world to use.

The calendar used internationally is based on the **Christian** calendar, which counts years from the birth of **Jesus** (taken as year 0). Other religions count years from events in their histories. For example, **Muslims** count years from the time the **Prophet Muhammad** migrated to **Madinah** – so, year 0 on the **Islamic** calendar is year 622 on the international calendar.

The international calendar has months that vary in length, making a year of 365 or 366 days. Some other calendars are based on lunar months of 29 or 30 days, making a year about 11 days shorter than an 'international' year. Some religions set the dates of **festivals** by their lunar calendar and so the festivals occur earlier each year on the international calendar. Because some festivals need to be in particular seasons, some religions using a lunar calendar add in an extra month every few years.
See also **AD, BC, BCE, CE**.

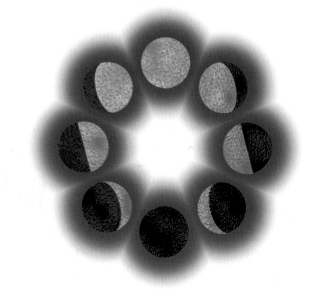

On a lunar calendar, the length of a month is based on the waxing and waning of the moon.

C

Candles are lit at an Advent ceremony in a church in the USA.

candle

Candles are part of many religious **services** and **festivals**. Their **light** is a **symbol** of the presence of **God** or the **gods**.

caste

Caste is the word used in English for the groups into which **Hindu** society is divided. The four main groups (called 'varnas') are: **Brahmins** (**priests**), Kshatriyas (soldiers), Vaishyas (merchants) and Shudras (labourers). These groups are divided into smaller groups called 'jatis'.

cathedral

A cathedral is the main **church** in an area (called a 'diocese') that is looked after by a **bishop**. It contains the bishop's throne or 'cathedra'.

St Basil's Cathedral in Moscow, built in the 16th century, is famous for its colourful onion-shaped domes.

Catholic

See **Roman Catholic**.

CE

CE stands for Common Era. It is often used instead of **AD**, as it is suitable for all religions.
See also **BC**, **BCE**, **calendar**.

ceremony

A ceremony is a set of actions performed in a particular, dignified way to celebrate or mark an occasion such as a **wedding** or **funeral**.

This chauri from northern India is made from yak hair and has a silver handle.

challah

Challah is a type of bread baked for **Shabbat** and other **Jewish festivals**.

On **Shabbat**, a day of rest, Jews have two loaves of bread. This reminds them of a story about their ancestors: in the desert after the **Exodus**, they received two days' worth of manna (bread) from **God**, so that they would not have to work at making bread on Shabbat.

chanting

Chanting is a way of half-speaking and half-singing words without musical accompaniment. The ancient **Buddhist scriptures** were passed down by **monks** through chanting, and **Buddhists** also use chanting to help them **meditate**. Some **Christians** use chanting in their **services**. **Hindu priests** chant verses from the scriptures at daily **worship** ('puja') and other **ceremonies**. **Jews** chant their scriptures.

Chanting helps Buddhists, like these nuns in Burma, to meditate.

charity

Charity means giving money or help to the poor. All religions encourage their followers to be aware of and help people in need.
See also **aqiqah**, **Id ul-Fitr**, **Islam**, **offerings**.

chauri

In **Sikh worship**, a chauri is a whisk or fan which is waved over the **Guru Granth Sahib** as a sign of respect. A chauri is made of long strands of yak hair, horse hair or nylon, attached to a silver or wooden handle.
See also **Sikhism**.

Christ

Christ is a title that was given to **Jesus** by people who believed that he was the **Messiah**, a special leader promised in the **Jewish** teachings.

Christian

Christian means to do with **Christianity**.

A Christian is someone who follows the teachings of **Jesus**. The worldwide community of Christians is called the Christian **Church**. Within it there are over 20,000 different groups or 'denominations', which interpret or practise their faith in different ways.
See also **Anglican**, **ecumenical movement**, **Orthodox Church**, **Pentecostal Christians**, **Protestant**, **Roman Catholic**.

Christianity

Christianity is the religion of **Christians**. They follow the teachings of **Jesus Christ**, a preacher and healer who lived 2,000 years ago in the land of **Israel** in the Middle East. Christians believe that Jesus was the son of **God** who came to earth to save people from their **sins**. After Jesus's death, his **disciples** spread his teachings far and wide. Today there are about three thousand million Christians and many kinds of Christian **churches**. Christianity is the world's largest religion.

Some Christians use a symbol of a fish, as a sign of their faith.

Believing in God

Christians believe in one God who created the world and watches over it. He is everywhere and sees and knows everything. Christians believe that God is kind and loving. He is always ready to **forgive** wrong-doing if the person is truly sorry and promises to follow Him.

Christians say that people can learn what God is like from Jesus's life and example. Most Christians believe that God can be seen in three ways: as God the Father, who made and cares for the world; as God the Son, who came to earth as Jesus; and as God, the **Holy Spirit** – meaning the power of God which is always at work in the world. Christians call these three persons in one God the Holy Trinity.

▷

The back of a silver cross made in Italy in the 15th century. The people pictured are the writers of the Gospels.

Jesus's life and teaching

In Jesus's time, the land of Israel and the **Jewish** people were ruled by the Romans. Jesus was born and brought up as a **Jew**. When he was 30 years old, Jesus began a new life. He travelled all over the country teaching people about God's love for them. He taught that people should love all others, including their enemies. 'Treat others as you would like them to treat you,' he said.

Death on the cross

Large crowds of people came to hear Jesus teach. He was popular with ordinary people, but the leaders of the Jewish religion did not like what he said. Three years after he started teaching, Jesus came to **Jerusalem** with his disciples. It was the time of the Jewish **festival** of **Pesach** (Passover). Jesus shared a meal with his disciples, which is known as the **Last Supper**. Then he went to a garden to pray. While he was there, soldiers came and arrested him. Jesus was charged with blasphemy (treating God's name with disrespect) because he called himself the Son of God. He was sentenced to death.

The next day, Jesus was crucified. He was nailed to a wooden cross and left to die. This is why the cross is such an important symbol for Christians. It reminds them of how and why Jesus died.

Rising from the dead

On the third day after he was crucified, Jesus rose from the dead. This is called the **Resurrection**. He appeared and spoke to his disciples several times after this. Then he was lifted into **heaven**, to be with God once more. This is called the **Ascension**. For Christians, the Resurrection and Ascension are very important. They believe that Jesus died to save people from their sins. They believe that if they follow Jesus and live a good life, they too will go to heaven when they die, to be with God.

Christian services

Christians **worship** God in many ways. On Sundays and at other special times, many Christians meet in a **church** for a **service** that includes **hymns**, **prayers** and readings from the **Bible**, the Christian holy book.

An important part of many Christian services is when worshippers remember the Last Supper by sharing some bread and wine. This ceremony has several different names, including Holy Communion, **Eucharist** and Mass. The **minister** or **priest** **blesses** the bread and wine and the worshippers eat a small piece of bread and take a sip of wine.

▽ Catholics at Easter Mass, at the cathedral in Beijing, China.

▷ God the Father (centre), Son (left) and Holy Spirit in a painting of the Trinity.

Christmas

Christmas is the **festival** when **Christians** remember the birth of **Jesus**. They thank **God** for His gift to the earth of Jesus, whom they believe was the Son of God.

The first Christians did not celebrate Jesus's birth. About 300 years afterwards, people began to celebrate his birth at the same time as a Roman sun festival. That is how Christmas came to be celebrated on 25 December. Some Christian **churches** celebrate Christmas in January.
See also **Advent, Christianity, Nativity**.

△

Many churches and schools put on a Nativity play, acting out the Christmas story.

church

A church is a building where **Christians worship**. Churches can be big or small, new or old, ornate or plain. The floor plan of many churches is in the shape of a cross. The word 'Church', often with a capital C, is also used to mean a group of Christians. For example: the Christian Church (Christians around the world), the **Anglican** Church (Christians from the Anglican tradition).
See also **cathedral, Christianity**.

circumcision

For **Jewish** and **Muslim** males, circumcision is a sign that they are part of their religious community. Circumcision means removing all or part of the foreskin (the loose skin at the end) from the penis. Jewish boys are circumcised at a **ceremony** called 'brit milah', when they are eight days old. Many Muslim boys are circumcised at a few days old. Some are circumcised later, up to the age of about ten.

confirmation

Many **Christian churches** hold confirmation **ceremonies** where Christians repeat for themselves the promises made for them at their **baptism**: to believe in and follow **Jesus**. They are then confirmed or accepted as full members of their church.

Confucius

Confucius (551-479 **BCE**) was a Chinese philosopher. He gave up his government job to teach people how to live in peace. He said they should practise these five virtues: kindness, goodness, modesty, wisdom and trustworthiness.

Today, there are about five million Confucians (followers of Confucius) in China and South East Asia.

◁

Confucius was famous for his wise sayings and writings.

congregation

A congregation is a group of people who meet for **worship**.

convent

A convent is a group of **Christian nuns**. It is also the building in which they live.

convert

A convert is a person who has changed from not following to following a religion, or from following one religion to following another.

'Convert' is also a verb: a person converts to a religion; or a person converts someone else to a religion.

covenant

A covenant is a two-way promise between **God** and a person or people, which makes their relationship stronger.
See also **ark**, **Judaism**.

cow

For **Hindus**, cows are **holy** animals. This is partly because cows give milk, a precious **food**. Hindus never hurt or kill cows, and do not eat beef. Cows are often seen wandering in Indian towns and cities.

Sometimes Hindus put garlands on cows.

Creation

For **Christians**, **Jews** and **Muslims**, the Creation means the making of the world by **God**. Stories of the Creation are told in the **Bible**, the **Torah** and the **Qur'an**.

creed

A creed is a short statement of **beliefs**.

cremation

Cremation is one type of **ceremony** that takes place after someone dies. The body of the person is burned to ashes. The ashes may be buried, or scattered in a special place. **Buddhists**, **Hindus** and **Sikhs** cremate their dead. Some **Christians** and **Jews** choose cremation rather than **burial**.
See also **afterlife**, **funeral**, **Ganges**, **reincarnation**.

crucifixion

For **Christians**, the Crucifixion means the death of **Jesus** on the cross. Crucifixion was the method used by the Romans for putting to death criminals who were not Roman citizens. The person was nailed to a cross and left until he suffocated.
See also **Christianity**, **Easter**, **Good Friday**.

cult

The word 'cult' is used to describe a religious group with its own leader, **rites** and **rituals**. Members of the group are often asked to cut themselves off from their families, to leave their friends and jobs, to make promises to stay with the group forever, to do whatever the leader says, and to give all their possessions to the group.

culture

Culture is the whole way of life of a group of people or of a region. Culture includes language, customs (such as to do with food or dress), **beliefs**, the people's ideas of right and wrong, the jobs people do, and the way they relate to each other. Most religions can be found in several cultures. Religion is usually practised differently in different cultures.

D

Dalai Lama

The Dalai Lama is the title of the chief **monk** (**lama**) of a main group of Tibetan **Buddhists**. The Dalai Lamas were religious leaders and also rulers of Tibet, from the mid-17th century until the Chinese invasion of Tibet in 1950.

The present Dalai Lama, Tenzin Gyatso (born in 1935), is the 14th Dalai Lama. Since 1959, he and many Tibetan Buddhists have lived in exile in India, because the Chinese government of Tibet does not allow Buddhists to practise their religion. The Dalai Lama travels the world, teaching about **Buddhism** and Tibet.

Tibetan Buddhists believe that the Dalai Lama is the **bodhisattva Avalokiteshvara** in human form.

Dassehra

Dassehra is a **Hindu festival**, held in September. In some parts of India it celebrates the victory of the **goddess** Durga over a **demon** in the shape of a buffalo. Here the festival is called Durga Puja. In other places, Hindus remember **Rama**'s victory over Ravana, a demon king. Travelling actors perform a play based on this story.
See also **Hinduism**, **Navaratri**, **Ramayana**.

Day of Judgement

Christians and **Muslims** believe that there will be a Day of Judgement when **God** will bring the dead back to life and judge each person. Those who have lived good lives on earth will stay with God forever, in peace and happiness. Those who have lived wicked lives will suffer in **hell**.
See also **afterlife**, **heaven**, **paradise**.

deity

A deity is another word for a **god** or **goddess**, or another **sacred** being.

On a visit to the USA, the Dalai Lama attends a ceremony for new monks.

A story tells of the Devil being thrown out of heaven. Sometimes devils are called 'fallen angels'.

demon

A demon is an **evil spirit** or **devil**. Some people say that demons bring bad into the world and make people behave badly.

devil

A devil is an **evil spirit** or **demon**. The Devil, with a capital D, is another name for **Satan**, the chief of the evil spirits.

devout

Devout means having a strong religious **belief** and being fully loyal to a religion.

Dhammapada

The Dhammapada is part of the **Tripitaka**, the **Theravada Buddhist scriptures**. It contains many of the **Buddha**'s sayings.

dharma

Dharma is an ancient Indian word meaning 'law' or 'teaching'. For **Hindus**, dharma is their 'duty', to look after **family** and friends, be honest and work hard. For **Buddhists**, the dharma (sometimes spelt 'dhamma') means the **Buddha**'s teaching.
See also **Buddhism**, **Hinduism**.

dialogue

A dialogue is a frank, open talk between two people or two groups. Dialogue between religions is often called inter-**faith** dialogue. This is a series of talks or even a relationship between people of different faiths, in which they try to understand each other better but not to change each other's **beliefs**.

disciple

Disciples are followers of a leader or teacher.

In the **Christian Bible**, the disciples are the 12 men whom **Jesus** chose to help him when he set out to teach and heal.
See also **apostle**, **Christianity**.

divine

Divine is another word for **sacred** or **holy**. It means to do with **God**, or with a **god** or **goddess**.

△

Diwali is the most important festival of the year for Hindus.

Diwali

Both **Hindus** and **Sikhs** have a Diwali **festival**, a festival of **light**, in October or November.

For many Hindus, Diwali is connected with the story from their **scriptures** of **Rama**, banished to the forest when he should have become king. After many battles, and helped by the monkey **god Hanuman**, Rama returns and takes his place on the throne. To guide him back from exile and celebrate his return, homes and **temples** are covered with lights.

Also at Diwali, Hindus say **prayers** to Lakshmi, the **goddess** of wealth, since Diwali marks the start of the new business year. There are fireworks, feasting, singing and dancing. People give each other sweets and other gifts, and everyone has new clothes.
See also **Ramayana**.

The Sikh Diwali festival remembers the release from prison of **Guru** Hargobind, who made sure that 52 Hindu princes were also freed with him. To celebrate the story, Sikhs light up the **Golden Temple** in **Amritsar**, and light lamps and **candles** in other places.
See also **Sikhism**.

Dome of the Rock

The Dome of the Rock is a building in **Jerusalem**. Inside is the sacred rock from which **Muslims** believe the **Prophet Muhammad** made his **Night Journey**.

◁

Many Muslims visit the Dome of the Rock. It is beautifully decorated in Islamic style.

dukkha

Dukkha is the word **Buddhists** use for 'suffering'. See **Buddhism**.

E

Easter

Easter is a **Christian festival** in March or April which celebrates the **resurrection** (rising from the dead) of **Jesus**. At many **church services** a **candle** or candles are lit, as a **symbol** of the risen Jesus. Because **Christianity's** central **belief** is in the Resurrection, Easter is the most important Christian festival.
See also **Good Friday, Holy Week, Lent, light, Palm Sunday**.

ecumenical movement

In the **Christian Church**, the ecumenical movement is a movement to bring together different denominations (groups) of Christians to **worship** and work together.

enlightenment

Enlightenment is an experience of realizing and understanding the truth. The word is associated particularly with **Buddhism**. **Buddhists** believe that Siddhartha Gautama (the **Buddha**) gained enlightenment at **Bodh Gaya**. Enlightenment is the aim of all Buddhists.
See also **Nirvana**.

A South Korean temple painting of the Buddha's enlightenment.

This Bible illustration of the Exodus shows the Egyptians drowning in the Red Sea.

Epiphany

Epiphany is a **Christian festival** marking the end of the **Christmas** period. It is held by most Christian **churches** on 6 January. For many Christians, the festival celebrates the visit of three wise men to the baby **Jesus**. For others, it celebrates the baptism of **Jesus** by **John the Baptist**.
See also **Nativity**.

etz hayim

For **Jews**, etz hayim (**Hebrew** for 'tree of life') is the wooden roller at each end of a **Torah** scroll.

Eucharist

Eucharist is one name for a **Christian ceremony** also known as Mass, the Lord's Supper and Holy Communion. Bread and wine are **blessed** and shared, in memory of the **Last Supper** when **Jesus** shared bread and wine saying, 'This is my body' and 'This is my blood'. The word 'Eucharist' can also mean the elements (the bread and wine) in the ceremony.
See also **Christianity**.

evil

Evil means wickedness or **sin**. It is the opposite of good.
See also **demon, devil, Satan**.

Exodus

The Exodus is a name given to the **Jewish** people's escape from slavery in Egypt, led by **Moses**. The book of Exodus in the **Bible** and the **Torah** tells the story of the escape. It tells how **God** sent ten plagues to persuade the Egyptian king to free the Jews; how the waters of the Red Sea were parted for the Jews to flee out of reach of Egyptian soldiers; and how Moses received the **Ten Sayings**.
See also **Judaism, Pesach**.

faith

Faith means **belief** or trust in **God** or in the teachings of a religion. Faith is also another word for 'religion'.

family

The family plays an important part in many religions, especially **Hinduism** and **Judaism**. Many **ceremonies** and **festivals** are celebrated at home.

In some religions, **God** or the **gods** are described by family names. For example, **Jews** and **Christians** often speak of God as their father and people as His children. Christians may see **Jesus** as their brother. Some **Hindus** refer to the **goddess** Durga as 'mother'.

fasting

Fasting means going without **food** or drink. In several religions, fasting is thought to be good for teaching people self-discipline and compassion.
See also **Islam**, **Lent**, **Ramadan**, **Yom Kippur**.

festival

A festival is a time of celebration, with **prayers** and **services**, processions, gifts and special **food**. Some religious festivals celebrate times of the year, such as new year, spring or harvest. Others remember a **deity** or a leader or an event from a religion's history.
See also **Advent**, **Baisakhi**, **calendar**, **Dassehra**, **Diwali**, **Easter**, **Epiphany**, **gurpurb**, **Hana Matsuri**, **Hanukkah**, **Holi**, **Id ul-Adha**, **Id ul-Fitr**, **Kathina**, **Losar**, **Pentecost**, **Pesach**, **Poya**, **Purim**, **Raksha Bandhan**, **Ramadan**, **Rosh Hashanah**, **Shabbat**, **Shavuot**, **Sukkot**, **Wesak**, **Yom Kippur**.

Five Ks

See **Sikhism**.

font

In a **Christian church**, a font is the basin containing the **water** used for **baptism**.

food

Food is shared at many religious celebrations. Sometimes foods are used as **symbols** to remind people of what a **festival** or celebration is about. Some religions have rules about food.
See also **challah**, **Eucharist**, **fasting**, **halal**, **haram**, **karah parshad**, **kashrut**, **langar**, **Pesach**.

forgive, forgiveness

To forgive means to excuse someone, and not be angry, for something he or she has done. **God**'s forgiveness is an important idea in several religions.
See also **Christianity**, **penance**, **Yom Kippur**.

Four Noble Truths

See **Buddhism**.

fundamentalist

A fundamentalist is a follower of a religion who believes that its **scriptures** are absolutely true and that its teachings should be strictly obeyed.

funeral

A funeral is a **ceremony** held to mark a person's death. It may include the person's **burial** or **cremation**.

At the festival of Baisakhi, Sikhs replace the flag at their gurdwara.

Gabriel

Gabriel (Jibril in **Arabic** and Gavriel in **Hebrew**) is an important **angel** in **Christianity**, **Islam** and **Judaism**. **Christians** believe that Gabriel foretold the birth of **Jesus**. **Muslims** believe that the **Prophet Muhammad** heard Jibril telling him to 'proclaim' the **Qur'an**.

Ganesha

Ganesha is a **Hindu god** with an elephant's head. Hindus pray to him to help them solve problems or when they start something new. He is also the god of travellers.

Ganges

For **Hindus** the Ganges is a **holy** river. They believe that a drop of its **water** can wash away their **sins**. They bathe in the river and scatter the ashes of their dead in its water.
See also **cremation**, **Hinduism**, **Varanasi**.

garland

A garland is a long necklace of flowers put round the neck of a **murti** in **Hindu worship**. Hindus also give garlands to guests as a sign of welcome.

God

In **Christianity**, **Islam**, **Judaism** and **Sikhism**, God is the one great, all-knowing power who created and cares for the world. In **Hinduism**, **Brahman** is sometimes known as God.
See also **Allah**.

god, goddess

Gods (male) and goddesses (female) are **sacred** beings or **spirits**.
See also **Brahma**, **Ganesha**, **Hinduism**, **Krishna**, **Rama**, **Shinto**, **Shiva**, **Vishnu**.

Good Friday

Good Friday is the day when **Christians** remember the **crucifixion** of Jesus.
See also **Easter**, **Holy Week**.

Golden Temple

The Golden Temple or 'Harimandir' in **Amritsar** is a very important building for **Sikhs**. It was built from marble and covered with copper and gold, decorated with verses from the **Guru Granth Sahib**.

The Golden Temple was built by Guru Arjan Dev, on a site where Guru Nanak, who started Sikhism, is said to have meditated.

Gospels

The Gospels are the first four books of the New Testament, part of the **Christian Bible**. Written by four early Christians, Matthew, Mark, Luke and John, the books tell of the life and teachings of **Jesus**.

For Hindus, putting a garland on someone is a sign of welcome.

granthi

A granthi is a **Sikh** appointed by a **gurdwara** to read from the **Guru Granth Sahib** at **services** and to perform **ceremonies**.

gurdwara

A gurdwara is a **Sikh** place of **worship**. Any place that contains a copy of the **Guru Granth Sahib** can be a gurdwara.
See also **langar, Nishan Sahib, Sikhism, takht**.

Gurmukhi

Gurmukhi is a script developed by the **Sikh Guru** Arjan Dev for writing Punjabi, the language in which the **Guru Granth Sahib** is written. 'Gurmukhi' means 'from the Guru's mouth'.

gurpurb

A gurpurb is a **Sikh festival** remembering the birth or death or an event in the life of one of the Sikh **Gurus**. All gurpurbs are marked by a non-stop reading aloud of the whole **Guru Granth Sahib**, by a team of readers. Important gurpurbs mark the birthdays of **Guru Nanak** and **Guru Gobind Singh** and the deaths of Guru Arjan Dev and Guru Tegh Bahadur (see **Sikhism**).

guru

For **Hindus**, a guru is a religious teacher.

For **Sikhs**, the word 'Guru' (always with a capital G) is used only for the ten Sikh Gurus who taught **Sikhism** between 1499 and 1708.

Guru Gobind Singh

Guru Gobind Singh was the tenth Sikh **Guru**, from 1675 to 1708. He began the **Khalsa**, the Sikh community.
See also **Sikhism**.

Guru Granth Sahib

The Guru Granth Sahib is the **holy** book of **Sikhism**. It was first put together as the **Adi Granth** by **Guru** Arjan Dev, including writings by himself, the Sikh Gurus before him and some **Hindu** and **Muslim** holy people. **Guru Gobind Singh** added the writings of the ninth Guru, and told Sikhs to call the book the Guru Granth Sahib. He said that the book would take the place of the human Gurus.

Every copy of the Guru Granth Sahib has 1,430 pages, with each **hymn** always on the same page number.
See also **chauri, granthi, gurdwara, Gurmukhi, Khalsa, Manji Sahib, rumala, takht**.

Guru Nanak

Guru Nanak (1469-1539) was the founder of **Sikhism** and the first Sikh **Guru**. He was brought up as a **Hindu** in northern India, at a time of conflict between Hindus and **Muslims**. When he was 30, a **revelation** from **God** led him to start a new religion based on the idea that everyone is equal in God's eyes.

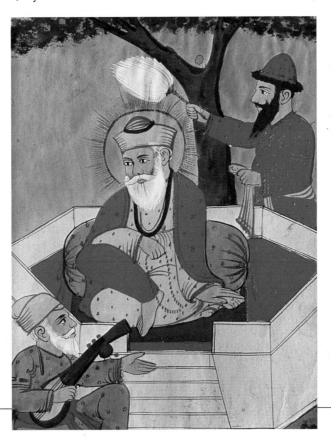

Guru Nanak with his Hindu friend Bala (right) and his Muslim friend Mardana (left).

25

H

Hadith

The Hadith are sayings of the **Prophet Muhammad**, which **Muslims** use to help them understand the teachings of the **Qur'an**. See also **Sunnah**.

hafiz

Hafiz is a title given to **Muslims** who have learned the whole of the **Qur'an** by heart.

Hajj

Hajj is the **pilgrimage** to **Makkah** that all **Muslims** try to make at least once in their lifetime. It takes place each year, in a month on the **Islamic calendar** called Dhul Hijjah. Pilgrims walk seven times around the **Ka'aba**. Then they walk or run between two hills called Safa and Marwa, remembering the story of Hagar, who ran searching for water for her son. Next the pilgrims go to Mount Arafat where the **Prophet Muhammad** preached his last **sermon**. At Mina they throw stones at three pillars which stand for **Satan**. They also celebrate the festival of **Id ul-Adha**. Finally they return to Makkah and again walk seven times around the Ka'aba. See also **Islam**, **Zamzam**.

halal

Halal, meaning 'allowed', describes **food** and drink that **Muslims** are permitted to eat. Fish, fruit and vegetables are halal. Pork is not. For other meat to be halal, the animal must be killed in a particular way. Muslim butchers sell halal meat.

halo

In paintings, a halo is a ring of **light** shown around the head of a figure who is believed to be **holy**, such as an **angel** or a **saint**.

Hana Matsuri

In Japanese **Buddhism**, Hana Matsuri is a flower **festival** celebrating the **Buddha's** birthday. **Temples** are decorated with cherry blossoms and children wear flowers in their hair. They visit the temple to pour sweet tea over a statue of the baby Buddha – remembering a story of the **gods** bathing the new-born Buddha with scented water.

At Hana Matsuri, sweet tea is poured over the Buddha statue.

Hanukkah

Hanukkah is a **Jewish festival** lasting for eight days in December. It remembers an event in ancient history when the **Jews** won back the **Temple** in **Jerusalem** from their enemies, who worshipped idols. The Jews found there was only enough oil to keep the Temple **menorah** burning for one day. But **God** kept the **light** burning for eight days, until more oil was found. At Hanukkah Jews light **candles**, one on the first night, two on the second, and so on until eight candles are lit on the last night. See also **Judaism**.

Hanuman

Hanuman is a **Hindu god** with the body of a monkey. In the **Ramayana**, Hanuman is a loyal general and friend of the god **Rama**. He leads the monkey army that helps Rama to rescue Sita. Hanuman is said to have magical powers, including being able to fly and change shape.

The monkey god Hanuman is believed to be very strong and brave.

hell

In many religions, hell is thought of as a terrible, miserable place to which the **souls** of wicked people go after death.
See also **afterlife**, **Day of Judgement**, **heaven**.

hijab

Worn by **Muslim** women, hijab is a scarf large enough to cover the head, neck and chest. The **Qur'an** tells Muslims to dress in a modest way. For women this means covering everything except their face, feet and hands.

Hijrah

The Hijrah ('departure') is the name that **Muslims** give to the **Prophet Muhammad's** migration from **Makkah** to **Madinah** in 622 **CE**. It was in Madinah that the Prophet established the first Muslim community, called the 'Ummah'. The Hijrah marks the start of the **Islamic calendar**.

Hindu

Hindu means to do with **Hinduism**.

A Hindu is someone who follows the religion of **Hinduism**. Hindus call their religion 'sanatana **dharma**' which means 'eternal law'.

haram

Haram, meaning 'forbidden', describes things that **Muslims** are not allowed to do. For example, drinking wine and eating pork are haram.
See also **Shari'ah**.

heaven

In many religions, heaven is thought of as a happy, peaceful place to which the **souls** of good people go after death. It is also the home of **God**, the **angels** or the **gods**.
See also **afterlife**, **Day of Judgement**, **hell**, **paradise**, **resurrection**.

Hebrew

Hebrew is the language in which the **Jewish scriptures** are written and it is the everyday language of **Israel**. Many **synagogues** run Hebrew classes.
See also **Judaism**.

▷

This is Psalm 114 written in Hebrew. It is part of a group of psalms known as 'Hallel' ('Praise'), sung especially at Jewish festivals.

Hinduism

Hinduism began about 4,000 years ago in India. It is a very varied religion, with many ways of **worshipping**, but most Hindus share the same main **beliefs**. Today, there are over 700 million Hindus. Most live in India but many have settled in other countries.

The great soul

Hindus believe in a great **soul** or **spirit**, called Brahman. Brahman cannot be seen, but is present in everything. A Hindu story explaining this tells of a wise man who was teaching his son about Brahman. He sprinkled some salt in some water and told the boy to take the salt out again. Of course this was impossible because the salt had dissolved. The wise man told his son that the salt had become like Brahman, invisible but everywhere.

△

Hindus bathe and worship in the River Ganges, at Varanasi. They call the Ganges the 'river of heaven'.

Gods and goddesses

There are thousands of Hindu **gods** and **goddesses**. Hindus believe that each one shows a different aspect of Brahman's power. The three most important gods are **Brahma**, the creator, **Vishnu**, the protector, and **Shiva**, the destroyer. Sometimes a god takes the form of a person or animal. This is called an **avatar**. Two avatars of Vishnu are **Krishna** and **Rama**. These two gods are worshipped all over India.

Hindus do not worship all the gods and goddesses. Some do not worship any at all. Others choose a particular god or goddess who is special to their family or who they believe has helped them in some way.

Birth, death and rebirth

Hindus believe that every person has his or her own soul, which is called 'atman'. They believe that when a person dies, his or her soul lives on and is born again ('reincarnated'). This can happen again and again, keeping the soul trapped in a cycle of birth, death and rebirth. The cycle is called 'samsara'. The aim of a Hindu's life is to escape from samsara and to reach 'moksha', or freedom. Then the soul, or atman, can join with Brahman. Each good action takes a person closer to moksha. Each wrong action takes a person further away. This is the law of **karma**.

◁

The Hindu goddess Durga kills a buffalo-shaped demon. This story is remembered at the Dassehra festival.

Going to the mandir

Hindu worship is called **puja**. Most Hindus have a small **shrine** at home. Some Hindus also go to worship at a **mandir** (**temple**), but there is no set day or time for worship. Some Hindus never go to the mandir at all. Others go only on **festivals**. Hindus decide on their own best way to worship and follow the customs of their family or community.

A mandir is a noisy, colourful place. Before they go in, Hindus take off their shoes as a sign of respect. Then they ring the temple **bell**. Hindus do not go to the mandir only to pray. They go to have a 'darshan' of the god or goddess. This means a sight of the **murti** (statue) which represents the god or goddess. They give the **priest** flowers, fruit and sweets to offer to the god or goddess, and afterwards the priest gives some of these offerings back to the worshippers as a sign of the god's or goddess's **blessing**. The priest also paints a red dot on the worshippers' foreheads. This is another mark of blessing.

This is aum (or 'om'), a sacred Hindu symbol. It represents a sound that Hindus chant at the beginning and end of prayers.

A special prayer

As part of puja, worshippers sing songs, say **prayers** and **chant** verses from the holy books. This short prayer is called the Gayatri Mantra. Hindus chant it in the morning, as the sun comes up.

Offerings are sold for Hindus to take in to the mandir.

'We **meditate** on the glory and brilliance of the sun god
Which lights up the heavens and the Earth.
May he bless us and inspire us.'

Holi

Holi is a **Hindu festival** in February or March. It marks the coming of spring. On the first day, some Hindus light a bonfire and burn a straw figure of a **demon**, Holika. In a Hindu story Holika tried to kill a prince who **worshipped Vishnu**. Vishnu saved the prince from the flames and Holika was burned instead. On the second day, people play practical jokes, including spraying each other with coloured water. This reminds them of **Krishna**'s mischievous childhood.

Paint-spraying at Holi is fun for Hindu children.

Jews in countries under Nazi rule were made to wear a distinctive badge like this 'Star of David' with 'Jew' ('Jude' in German) inside it.

Holocaust

The Holocaust is the name given to the mass murder of **Jews** by the Nazis during the Second World War (1939-45). Six million Jews from Europe, and two million other people including gypsies and people with disabilities, were killed. The **Hebrew** name for the Holocaust is 'Shoah'. Jews observe a Holocaust memorial day ('Yom HaShoah') each year in April.

holy

Holy means separate or set apart for a special purpose. It is another word for **divine** or **sacred**.

Holy Communion

See **Eucharist**.

Holy Spirit

For **Christians**, the Holy Spirit is the mysterious power of **God** at work in people and in the world. It is often represented as breath or wind, as fire, or as a white dove.
See also **Christianity**, **Pentecost**.

Holy Week

For **Christians**, Holy Week is the week that leads up to **Easter**. It starts with **Palm Sunday**, named after the story of **Jesus** riding into **Jerusalem** on a donkey and being welcomed by people waving palm branches. Many Christian **churches** act out this story.

On the Thursday of Holy Week, called Maundy Thursday, Christians remember the **Last Supper**. On the following day, called **Good Friday**, they remember the **crucifixion** of Jesus. Many Christians take part in processions, carrying a cross.
See also **Christianity**.

horoscope

A horoscope is a chart showing the position of the stars and planets at a particular moment. Some people believe that horoscopes for the time of a person's birth tell something about that person's character, and that horoscopes can be interpreted to predict the future. Many **Hindus** use horoscopes to choose a date for an important event, such as a wedding.

huppah

A huppah is a canopy under which a **Jewish** wedding **ceremony** takes place. The canopy is a **symbol** of the openness of the home.

hymn

A hymn is a song of praise. **Christians**, **Hindus**, **Jews** and **Sikhs** sing hymns as part of **worship**.
See also **psalm**.

I

Ibrahim

See **Abraham**.

Id ul-Adha

Id ul-Adha ('**festival** of **sacrifice**') is marked by **Muslims** at the end of the month of pilgrimage (**Hajj**). It remembers how the **Prophet Ibrahim**, ready to obey **Allah** even by sacrificing his son, received a ram from Allah to sacrifice instead. At Id ul-Adha, Muslims on Hajj sacrifice a sheep or a goat. Muslims elsewhere often sacrifice an animal and share the meat with the poor.

Id ul-Fitr

Id ul-Fitr is a **festival** celebrated by **Muslims** at the end of **Ramadan**. It is marked with **prayers** and parties and by giving money to **charity**.

ik onkar

See **Mool Mantra**.

Imam

An Imam is a **Muslim** who teaches and leads the **mosque** community. He leads **prayers**, and gives a talk at Friday (**jumu'ah**) midday prayers. 'Imam' is also a title used by **Shi'a** Muslims for 12 leaders of the Muslim community.

 An Imam speaks to the congregation at a mosque in Algeria.

Islamic

Islamic means to do with, or based on, **Islam**.

Israel

Israel is a name for the **Jewish** people and for their homeland. The people of Israel originated in the land of Israel about 3,000 years ago. **Jews** believe that they belong with the land and that God promised it to them. In 1948, Israel became an independent Jewish state.
See also **Jerusalem**, **Judaism**, **Zionism**.

Islam

Followers of Islam are called **Muslims**. The word Islam means 'obedience'. Muslims obey the will of **Allah (God)** and follow His guidance in all parts of their lives.

Muslims believe that Islam started with Adam, the first man. They believe that Adam was the first of many **prophets** (messengers) sent by Allah to teach people how to live and **worship** Him. They believe that their religion was 'completed' by the last and greatest prophet, the Prophet **Muhammad**, who was born in **Makkah** in Arabia (now Saudi Arabia) about 1,400 years ago. Allah revealed His message to the Prophet Muhammad in **Arabic** and it was written down to form the **Qur'an**.

After the Prophet Muhammad's death, Islam spread far and wide. Today, there are about one thousand million Muslims in the world and Islam is the fastest-growing religion. The worldwide community of Muslims is called the 'Ummah'.

△

A symbol of Islam consists of a star and a crescent moon.

▽

Muslim pilgrims dress in white for the Hajj. They gather in the Grand Mosque in Makkah, in the centre of which is the Ka'aba.

Allah

The most important **belief** of Islam is the belief that Allah is the one true God who created the world and everything in it. Allah has no parents, partner or children. No one created Allah. He has always been there. He is all-powerful, all-seeing and all-knowing. There are ninety-nine names for Allah in the Qur'an. For example, he is the Merciful, the Forgiver, the Generous and the Kind.

The Five Pillars

The Five Pillars of Islam are five practices that Muslims follow. Just as real pillars support, or hold up, a building, so these practices support Islam.

- Saying the *Shahadah*. This is a sentence that sums up what Muslims believe. It says, 'There is no god except Allah, and Muhammad is the Prophet of Allah.'

- *Salah*. This means **prayer**. Muslims pray in Arabic, five times a day: at dawn, midday, mid-afternoon, just after sunset and night.

- *Zakah*. This means giving money to the poor and needy. All Muslims who have savings must give a part of this money each year as zakah.

- *Sawm*. This means **fasting** in daylight hours in the month of **Ramadan**. By fasting, people learn self-discipline. They also gain a greater understanding of how people who are really hungry and starving must feel, and of how great a gift food is.

- *Hajj*. This means making a **pilgrimage** to the **holy** city of Makkah. Muslims try to do this at least once in their lives.

Prayer

Muslims can pray anywhere, provided that the place is clean. If they are going to be where the ground may be dirty, they take a prayer mat called a **sajjadah** with them. Before they pray, Muslims wash their face, hands and feet in a **ritual** way called **wudhu**. Then, to say their prayers, they face towards Makkah. As they say the words of the prayers, they move through a series of prayer positions called **rak'ahs**.

Going to a mosque

Some Muslims choose to go to a **mosque** to say their daily prayers. But on Fridays all Muslims try to go to the mosque for midday prayers and to listen to a talk by the **Imam**.

People must take off their shoes before they go into the mosque, and inside, men and women sit apart. All mosques have a special washing area for wudhu. Larger mosques may have other rooms such as a library, a kitchen, a hall, and classrooms for **madrasahs**.

△

As they pray, Muslims move through a set of prayer positions. Kneeling, with palms and forehead touching the floor, this man says, in Arabic, 'Glory to my God, in the Highest'.

▷

Learning to read Arabic at a madrasah in Nigeria.

J

Jain

A Jain is someone who follows the teachings of a holy man known as Mahavira, who lived in India in the 6th century **BCE**. Today there are thought to be about 3.5 million Jains, most of whom live in western India. Jains share many **beliefs** with **Hindus** and **Buddhists**, for instance in the idea of **karma**. They believe that they can achieve freedom from the cycle of birth, death and rebirth by leading an austere (strict) life and especially by **ahimsa** – behaving so that no living creature is harmed.

These paintings from Thailand depict scenes from some Jataka tales.

Jataka tale

A Jataka tale is a type of story often used to teach **Buddhists** about the ideas of the **Buddha** and to guide them in their behaviour. The tales are about the Buddha's past lives, which he was able to remember because he had reached **enlightenment**. In some of the tales, the Buddha is born as an animal.

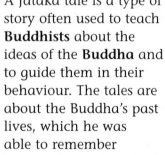

Jerusalem

Jerusalem is a city in **Israel** that is sacred to **Christians**, **Jews** and **Muslims**.
For Christians, it is where **Jesus** spent his last days on earth and was crucified.
For Jews, who also call it '**Zion**', it was the ancient capital of the Promised Land. It is also the capital of modern Israel.
For Muslims, it is the place from which the **Prophet Muhammad** began his miraculous **Night Journey**.
See also **Christianity, Dome of the Rock, Judaism, temple, Western Wall.**

A Gospel story tells that the disciples Peter, James and John saw Jesus talking with the prophets Moses and Elijah. This picture of the story was painted by Duccio di Buoninsegna

Jesus

Christians believe that Jesus, who lived about 2,000 years ago in the land of **Israel**, was the Son of **God**. They believe he was the **Messiah** that God had promised to send to earth, and that, by his death and **resurrection**, he saved people from their **sins**.
For **Muslims**, Jesus (Isa in **Arabic**) is a **prophet**.
See also **apostle, Christ, Christianity, Christmas, disciple, John the Baptist, Nativity.**

John the Baptist

For **Christians**, John the Baptist was the cousin of **Jesus**. Before Jesus started teaching, John preached to people and **baptized** them in the River Jordan, as a **symbol** of washing away their **sins**. Jesus asked to be baptised by John and afterwards, according to the **Gospel** story, **God**'s voice was heard saying, 'This is my Son, my Beloved, on whom my favour rests.'

Joseph

The **Christian** and **Jewish scriptures** include the story of Joseph. His father, Jacob, gave him a beautiful coat, which made his brothers jealous. They sold Joseph as a slave and told Jacob that he was dead. Joseph was taken to Egypt where eventually the Pharaoh put him in charge of sharing out grain supplies during a famine. Joseph later forgave his brothers and was reunited with Jacob.

Another Joseph is important to **Christians** as the earthly father of **Jesus**. He was a carpenter from Nazareth. See also **Mary**, **Nativity**.

There is a popular musical show based on the story of Joseph and his beautiful coat.

Jew

A Jew is someone who belongs to the **Jewish** people. The religion of these people is **Judaism**. Different groups of Jews practise Judaism in different ways. **Orthodox** Jews follow the laws of the **Torah** very strictly. **Progressive** Jews believe that Judaism needs to change so as to fit in with modern life.

Jewish

Jewish means to do with **Judaism**. The Jewish people are descendants of **Abraham**. See also **Israel**.

jihad

'Jihad' is **Arabic** for 'effort' or 'challenge'. For **Muslims** the word describes their personal struggle against **evil** or **temptation**, any effort they make for good, and any battle fought to defend **Islam**. There are rules for such battle, including that no women or children may take part and that fighting must stop as soon as the enemy surrenders.

jumu'ah

For **Muslims**, jumu'ah is Friday: the day when there is a talk by the **Imam** during midday **prayers** at the **mosque**. All Muslims try to go to the mosque at this time of the week. See also **Islam**, **khutbah**.

Judaism

Judaism is the religion of the **Jewish** people. According to the **Torah** (part of the Jewish **scriptures**), the first Jew was **Abraham**, who lived in the Middle East more than 4,000 years ago. He belonged to a group of nomadic (wandering) people called the Hebrews. Abraham is called the father of the Jewish people. He taught the Jews to **worship** one **God**, instead of many different gods.

The Star of David, a symbol of Judaism.

Today, there are about 13 million Jews. They live all over the world but mostly in the USA, **Israel** and Europe.

The Jewish people

Jews believe in one God who is eternal, all-seeing and all-knowing. He made the world and looks after it. They believe that God made a **covenant** with Abraham. God said that Abraham and his descendants (now called the Jews) should always worship only Him. Then He would look after the Jews for ever and give them a land to live in, the land called Canaan (which we now call Israel). This is sometimes referred to as 'the Promised Land'.

Abraham and his family settled in Canaan, but a famine forced their descendants to move to Egypt. They worked for the Egyptians, but soon became slaves and, for 400 years, their lives were very miserable. God told a man called **Moses** to help the Jews leave Egypt. Their escape is called the **Exodus** and Jews believe it was a **miracle**. After 40 years in the desert, where God gave them the **Ten Sayings**, they finally reached the Promised Land.

Candles are lit in windows at Hanukkah, a festival which remembers the ancient Jews winning back the Temple from their enemies in 168 BCE.

On the table for Shabbat are candles, wine or grape juice, and two loaves of bread called challah.

Jews believe that God chose them to receive the Torah and to pass on to other people its teachings about justice, peace, kindness and truth. They also believe that God gave them some commandments, called **mitzvot**, which only they need to keep.

Jewish worship

Jews can worship on their own and in any place, but usually they pray with other Jews, mostly at home but also at the **synagogue**. There are three **prayer** times a day: evening, morning and afternoon. (There are also prayers for waking up and going to sleep.)

Each week Jews have a day of rest called **Shabbat**. It lasts from Friday evening to Saturday evening. The **family**, often with guests, takes three Shabbat meals together. Many Jews go to synagogue on Shabbat, to hear the reading or **chanting** of the Torah. They also spend time relaxing with their family and friends. Family life is precious to Jews.

Prayer items

Some Jews wear special clothes when they pray. The following items are usually worn by men:

Kippah – a skull cap. (Another name for this is a 'yarmulke'.) Covering the head shows respect for God. Some Jews wear a kippah all the time, not just for worship.

Tallit – a prayer shawl. It is made of wool or silk, and has fringes at each end. The prayer shawl reminds the person wearing it to obey God.

To show respect for God, and to help him pray, this man has put on his kippah, tallit and tefillin.

The Shema, written on a tiny scroll, is put inside the mezuzah, a small box which Jews fix to the doorposts of their homes.

Tefillin – two small leather boxes. One is placed on the middle of the forehead and kept in place with a strap. The other is tied to the arm, pointing at the heart. Inside the boxes are tiny scrolls on which passages from the Torah are written. The tefillin remind Jews to love God with all their heart and mind.

The Shema

The most important Jewish prayer is called the Shema. It begins:

'Hear, O Israel, the Lord is our God. The Lord is One. Love the Lord your God with all your heart, and with all your soul, and with all your might.'

K

Ka'aba

The Ka'aba is a cube-shaped building in the Grand **Mosque** in **Makkah**. **Muslims** believe that it was built by **Ibrahim** and his son Isma'il, as a place for people to **worship Allah**. Wherever they are in the world, Muslims turn to face the Ka'aba when they pray.
See also **Hajj, Islam, salah.**

kacch

See **Sikhism**.

Muslims on Hajj (pilgrimage) walk seven times around the Ka'aba. It is covered in a black cloth, embroidered in gold with words from the Qur'an.

kanga

See **Sikhism**.

kara

See **Sikhism**.

karah parshad

Karah parshad is a **food** made of semolina, flour, sugar, butter or ghee (clarified butter) that is shared out at the end of **Sikh services** to show that everyone is equal.

karma

Important in **Buddhism**, **Hinduism** and **Jainism**, karma is the idea that all a person's actions, good or bad, have their effects on the person's present life and on his or her rebirth.

kashrut

Kashrut is a set of **food** laws followed by **Jews**. Found in the **Torah**, the laws describe foods as either 'kasher' (or 'kosher') – right to eat, or 'tref'.

Kathina

Kathina is a **Theravada Buddhist festival** held in November, when Buddhists take gifts, especially cloth for new robes, to the **monks** in their local **vihara** (**monastery**).

Kaur

Kaur ('princess') is a **name** given to every **Sikh** female. So a Sikh girl might be called Mandeep Kaur (followed often by her family name).
See also **Khalsa, Singh**.

kes

See **Sikhism**.

Khalsa

The Khalsa ('the Pure') is the **Sikh** community started by **Guru Gobind Singh** in 1699. As a test, the Guru asked five times for the head of a Sikh willing to die for his **beliefs**. Five men offered themselves. The Guru did not kill them, but made them the first members of the Khalsa by giving them **amrit** (a mixture of sugar and water, stirred with a two-edged sword). He gave the **names Singh** ('Lion') to men and **Kaur** ('Princess') to women who joined the Khalsa; and he told them all to wear the Five Ks (see **Sikhism**). Sikhs today still join the Khalsa by taking amrit at a special **ceremony**.
See also **Baisakhi, Panj Piarey**.

khanda

The khanda is a **Sikh symbol** made up of a two-edged sword (standing for **God**'s power as creator), a circle (standing for continuity) and two swords (standing for spiritual and earthly power). One place where the khanda symbol is always used is on the Sikh flag, the **Nishan Sahib**.

The khanda symbol.

khutbah

The khutbah is a talk given by the **Imam** at Friday **prayers** in a **mosque**. See also **Islam, jumu'ah**.

kirpan

See **Sikhism**.

kosher

See **kashrut**.

Krishna

Krishna is a popular **Hindu god**. In one story about him, he lifts up a mountain to shelter his friends from a downpour of rain. There are also many stories of his love of mischief and playing tricks on his friends.

Krishna is usually represented with dark blue or black skin, and playing a flute. His wife is a beautiful milkmaid called Radha. See also **Bhagavad Gita, Hinduism, Holi**.

lama

A lama ('teacher') is a **monk** in Tibetan **Buddhism**. The **Dalai Lama** is the chief one. Since the Chinese invasion of Tibet in 1950, many lamas have moved to Europe and the USA, where they teach people about their **faith**. Tibetan Buddhism has many **rituals**. For some, the monks wear bright costumes and play unusual musical instruments.

See also **bhikkhu, Losar, Mahayana, mandala**.

Tibetan Buddhist monks, or 'lamas', normally wear maroon robes.

langar

The langar ('**Gurus**' kitchen') is a kitchen or dining hall of a **gurdwara**, where everyone shares a meal after attending a **Sikh service**. The meal itself is also called langar.

All members of the gurdwara take turns to prepare and serve the **food**, which is always vegetarian. Anyone is welcome to take langar, which expresses the Sikh idea that all people are equal.

Last Supper

For **Christians**, the Last Supper is a meal that **Jesus** ate with his **disciples** on the day before he was **crucified**. They remember the Last Supper in a **service** called **Eucharist**.

lectern

In a **church**, a lectern is a stand from which the **Bible** is read.

Jesus and his disciples at the Last Supper.

legend

A legend is a story about a person, a people or a place that may have existed a long time ago. Legends are an important part of people's understanding of their religion's beginnings and purpose.

Lent

For **Christians**, Lent is a period of 40 days from **Ash Wednesday** to the day before **Easter**. During Lent Christians prepare for Easter by spending more time than usual in **prayer** and **Bible** study. They also remember a story about **Jesus** spending 40 days in the desert before he started to preach. In the desert, the **Devil** tempted Jesus to think more of himself than of **God**'s wishes. But Jesus resisted the Devil's **temptation**. To understand how it feels to resist temptation, some Christians go without something they enjoy, such as sweets, for Lent. See also **Shrove Tuesday**.

lesson

A lesson is a passage from the **Bible** read aloud during a **Christian service**.

light

Light is a **symbol** of the presence of **God** or the **gods**. It is used in **worship** to give a feeling of **spiritual** understanding, warmth and energy. See also **Advent**, **arti**, **Buddhism**, **candle**, **Diwali**, **Easter**, **halo**, **Hanukkah**, **menorah**, **Ner Tamid**, **Wesak**.

Lord's Prayer

The Lord's Prayer is a **prayer** said by **Christians** in private and at most **church services**. It is based on a prayer that **Jesus** taught to his **disciples**. It begins 'Our Father, who is in heaven, Hallowed be Your name'.

Losar

Losar is a Tibetan **Buddhist festival** marking the new year. People spring-clean their homes and light torches and firecrackers to scare away **evil spirits**. They visit **monasteries** with gifts for the **monks**, and give money and food to the poor. A highlight of Losar is a butter sculpture competition among the monks.

lotus flower

Lotuses grow in ponds and rivers, but their flowers bloom above the surface of the water. **Buddhists** say that people who follow the **Buddha**'s teaching to reach **enlightenment** rise above life's sufferings as lotus flowers rise above the water. The **Sikh scriptures** say that as the lotus flower stays dry, so a person should live untouched by the world.

For **Hindus**, a lotus is a **symbol** of **Vishnu**, who was born from a lotus flower.

M

Madinah

Madinah in Saudi Arabia is the second most **holy** city of **Islam** after **Makkah**. The **Prophet Muhammad** migrated from Makkah to Madinah in 622 **CE** and started the first **Muslim** community there. The Prophet died in the city in 632 and is buried there. See also **Hijrah**.

madrasah

A madrasah is a class held in a **mosque** where **Muslim** children and young people learn to recite the **Qur'an** in **Arabic**. They also learn the **Islamic** way of praying. Children start going to the madrasah from about the age of four.

Mahabharata

The Mahabharata is part of the **Hindu scriptures**. It is the world's longest poem, with 100,000 verses. The most popular part is the **Bhagavad Gita**.

Mahayana Buddhism

Mahayana Buddhism is one of two main types of **Buddhism**. The other is **Theravada**. Mahayana includes Tibetan Buddhism, **Pure Land**, **Zen** and other types of Buddhism that developed from the first century **CE**. Mahayana **Buddhists** believe in many **Buddhas** and **bodhisattvas**.

Makkah

Makkah in Saudi Arabia is the most **holy** city of **Islam**. It is where the **Prophet Muhammad** was born and received the words of the **Qur'an**. See also **Hajj**, **Ka'aba**.

mandala

A mandala is a circular picture which Tibetan **Buddhists** use to help them **meditate**. In their minds they follow a way from the edge to the centre of the picture, like following a map. In Tibet, **monks** make mandalas from sand, butter and even modelling clay.

Tibetan Buddhist monks in the USA made this mandala out of coloured sand.

A 14th-century Russian painting of Mary and Jesus.

mandir

A mandir is a place where **Hindus worship**. It is also called a **temple**. A mandir is dedicated to one or more **gods** or **goddesses**, and is seen as the home on earth of those **deities**. See also **bell**, **Hinduism**, **murti**.

Manji Sahib

The Manji Sahib is a set of three cushions and a quilt on which Sikhs place and open the **Guru Granth Sahib**.

martyr

A martyr is someone who willingly suffers and even dies for his or her religious **beliefs**.

Mary

For **Christians**, Mary was the person chosen by **God** to be the mother of His son, **Jesus**. Mary is particularly important to **Orthodox Christians** and **Roman Catholics**, who often pray to her as 'Our Lady'. Many Roman Catholic **churches** have statues or pictures of Mary. See also **Bethlehem**, **Christmas**, **Gabriel**, **Joseph**, **Nativity**.

Mass

See **Eucharist**.

matriarch

A matriarch is an important mother figure in a **family** or community. In the history of the **Jewish** people, Sarah, Rebecca, Rachel and Leah are described as matriarchs. See also **Judaism**, **patriarch**.

Mecca

See **Makkah**.

Medina

See **Madinah**.

This is a menorah shown as part of a stained-glass window at a synagogue in Jerusalem.

meditate, meditation

To meditate means to concentrate one's mind on just one idea or to try to clear one's mind of all thoughts. The aim of meditation may be to achieve deeper understanding or a feeling of calm. Learning to meditate takes lots of practice, because it is hard to stop the mind being distracted by many thoughts and ideas. Meditation is used in several religions. It is very important in **Buddhism**.

menorah

A menorah is a candlestick with seven branches, and has become the **symbol** of **Judaism**. In ancient times, a golden menorah was lit every day in the **Temple** in **Jerusalem**. Its light was a sign of **God**'s presence. Today, the official symbol of **Israel** is a menorah.

Messiah

In the **Jewish scriptures** and in the **Old Testament** of the **Christian Bible**, the Messiah is a promised leader. The scriptures say that this leader will come from the descendants of King David (who died c.962 **BCE**) and establish **God**'s kingdom on earth. **Christians** believe that **Jesus** was the promised Messiah. **Jews** believe that the Messiah is still to come. See also **Christ**.

metta

Metta is a **Buddhist** word for loving kindness. It is one of four qualities that the **Buddha** called the highest states of mind. The others are compassion, joy in the happiness of others, and calm acceptance of whatever happens.

Metta Sutta

Part of the **Tripitaka**, the Metta Sutta is the **Buddha**'s teaching about **metta**. It begins, 'May all beings be happy, whoever they are.' See also **sutra**.

mezuzah

A mezuzah is a small box that **Jews** fix to the doorposts of their homes. The box contains a tiny piece of parchment on which is written a Jewish **prayer** called the **Shema** (see **Judaism**). Many Jews touch the mezuzah and kiss their fingers as they go in and out of their home.

Middle Way

The Middle Way is another name for the Noble Eightfold Path (see **Buddhism**).

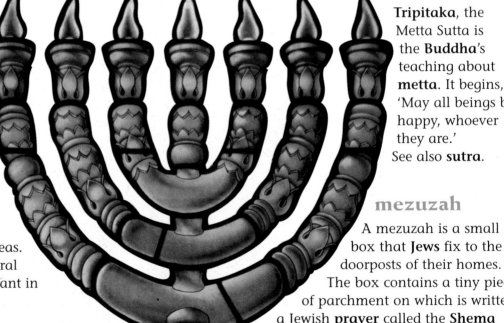

mihrab

In a **mosque**, the mihrab is a niche or alcove in one wall. It is positioned so that by facing towards it when they pray, **Muslims** face in the direction of the **Ka'aba**. See also **Islam**.

minaret

A minaret is a tall tower on a **mosque**, from which the **adhan** (call to **prayer**) is made.

The decoration on this minaret is an example of Islamic art, using calligraphy and geometric patterns. ▷

minbar

In a **mosque**, the minbar is a platform from which the **Imam** gives a talk (**khutbah**) at the Friday midday **prayers**. See also **Islam**, **jumu'ah**.

minister

A minister is a general name for someone appointed to lead **services** in the **Christian Church**. Different churches use different words for their ministers, including parson, **priest** and **vicar**.

miracle

A miracle is an amazing event which cannot be explained by any law of nature. Miracles include healing people from diseases, without medicines or operations, and unusual events in nature. Miracles are often seen as a sign of the power of **God** or the **gods**.

missionary

A missionary is someone who sets out to teach other people about his or her religion and, especially, to spread that religion to other places. There are missionaries in **Buddhism**, **Christianity** and **Islam**. See also **convert**.

mitzvah, mitzvot

For Jews, a mitzvah (plural: mitzvot) is a commandment from **God**. Sometimes 'mitzvah' is used to mean a good deed. See also **Judaism**, **Ten Sayings**.

moksha

In **Hinduism**, moksha means freedom from the cycle of birth, death and rebirth called **samsara**. See also **dharma**.

monastery

A monastery is a place where **monks** live, **worship** and study. See also **convent**, **vihara**.

▽

The Christian monastery of St Catherine on Mount Sinai, Egypt.

monk

In **Buddhism** and **Christianity**, a monk is a man who has devoted himself to his religion and vowed to follow the way of life of a particular religious community. Different communities of **Christian** monks are called 'Orders'. Each has its own rules and a main activity, such as education.
See also **bhikkhu**, **monastery**, **nun**, **Sangha**, **vihara**.

Mool Mantra

The Mool Mantra is the opening verse of the **Guru Granth Sahib**, recited by **Sikhs** as part of their **worship**. It begins 'There is only one **God**'. The **Gurmukhi** script for those words makes a Sikh **symbol** known as 'ik onkar'.

Moses

Moses was a **Jewish** leader, whose story is told in the **Christian** and **Jewish scriptures**. He was born about 3,200 years ago in Egypt, where the **Jews** were slaves. The king of Egypt wanted to kill all Jewish baby boys, but Moses was saved. As a young man, he received a **revelation** from **God**, telling him to lead the Jews out of slavery to the 'Promised Land'. On the way, God appeared to Moses on Mount Sinai and gave him the **Ten Commandments** (or **Ten Sayings**) and the **Torah**.

Moses (in **Arabic**, Musa) is one of the **prophets** mentioned in the **Qur'an**.
See also **Exodus**, **Israel**, **Judaism**.

mosque

A **mosque** (in **Arabic**, masjid) is a building where **Muslims worship** and meet. Many mosques have a dome-shaped roof and one or more **minarets** and are decorated with patterns and verses from the **Qur'an**. But mosques around the world can look quite different.
See also **adhan**, **Imam**, **Islam**, **jumu'ah**, **madrasah**, **mihrab**, **minbar**, **wudhu**.

muezzin

In **Islam**, a muezzin is a **Muslim** who makes the call to **prayer** (**adhan**) from a **mosque**.

Muhammad, the Prophet

Muslims believe that the **Prophet** Muhammad was the last and greatest of many prophets sent by **Allah** to teach people how to live. He was born in 570 **CE** in **Makkah**. The people there had forgotten Allah and **worshipped** idols. One night in the month of **Ramadan** in 610, the Prophet heard a voice saying 'Proclaim' (tell). It was the voice of the **angel** Jibril (**Gabriel**) giving him Allah's message to tell to others. This happened many more times over the next 23 years. The words revealed to the Prophet were written down to form the **Qur'an**.

▽

The many minarets of the Suleimaniye Mosque in Istanbul, Turkey, are typically tall, slim and pencil-shaped.

In 622 **CE** the Prophet moved to **Madinah**, where he started the first **Islamic** community. He died in 632. See also **Dome of the Rock**, **Hijrah**, **Islam**, **Night Journey**, **Night of Power**.

N

In the Nativity story the wise men follow a star, which leads them to the baby Jesus.

names

Many parents name their children after people in the stories and histories of their religion. For **Christian** and **Jewish** parents in particular, there are naming **ceremonies** for babies, which introduce the child to the community.

A **Sikh** baby's first name is chosen by opening the **Guru Granth Sahib** at random and deciding on a name beginning with the first letter of the first word on the left-hand page. See also **aqiqah**, **baptism**, **Kaur**, **Singh**.

Nativity

For **Christians**, the Nativity means the birth of **Jesus**. The Nativity story tells that Jesus was born in a stable in **Bethlehem**, and that shepherds and wise men brought him gifts. See also **Christmas**, **Epiphany**, **Joseph**, **Mary**.

Navaratri

Navaratri (meaning 'nine nights') is a **Hindu festival**, when the mother **goddess** Durga is **worshipped** – especially by performing 'stick dances' and songs in praise of the goddess. Navaratri is also called **Dassehra**.

murti

In **Hinduism**, a murti is an image (a statue or a picture) of a **god** or **goddess**. Murtis are treated with great respect in **Hindu worship**, both at home and in a **mandir**. They are washed in water or milk, dressed in red and gold and given **garlands**. **Offerings** are made to them and the **arti** lamp is waved in front of them.

A murti of the god Ganesha.

Muslim

A Muslim is someone who follows the religion of **Islam**. There are two main groups of Muslims, the **Sunni** and the **Shi'a**. See also **Sufi**.

myth

A myth is a story that explains, in an imaginative way, something in nature or human life which is confusing or mysterious.

Ner Tamid

The Ner Tamid ('eternal light') is a light that hangs above the **ark** in a **synagogue**. **Jews** keep this **light** always shining, as a reminder of the **menorah** which was lit every day in the **Temple** in Jerusalem.

New Testament

See **Bible**.

Night Journey

For **Muslims**, the Night Journey ('Laylat ul-Miraj') is a miraculous event in the life of the **Prophet Muhammad**. The Prophet described what happened. He was taken by the **angel** Jibril (**Gabriel**) from **Makkah** to **Jerusalem**. Here he met all the earlier prophets. Then he travelled up through the **heavens** to the throne of **Allah**. Allah gave him the five daily **prayer** times for Muslims to observe. Then the Prophet returned to Makkah.
See also **Dome of the Rock, Islam**.

Night of Power

For **Muslims**, the Night of Power ('Laylat ul-Qadr') is the night in **Ramadan** when the **Prophet Muhammad** first heard the **angel** Jibril (**Gabriel**) and began to speak the words from **Allah** which became the **Qur'an**. Some Muslims today spend this night praying and reading the Qur'an.

Nirvana

In **Buddhism**, Nirvana is a state of perfect peace and happiness reached by people who gain **enlightenment** and become free from the cycle of birth, death and rebirth. See also **afterlife, reincarnation**.

Nishan Sahib

The Nishan Sahib is the **Sikh** flag, flown at all **gurdwaras** and buildings of Sikh organizations. The flag is triangular and yellow, with the **khanda symbol** on it.

Noah

In the **Christian** and **Jewish scriptures**, Noah is a man whom **God** tells to build an **ark**, to save his family and two of each animal from a flood. In the **Qur'an**, Noah (Nuh, in **Arabic**) is one of the **prophets**.

Noble Eightfold Path
See **Buddhism**.

Noble Truths
See **Buddhism**.

nun

In **Buddhism** and **Christianity**, a nun is a woman who has devoted herself to her religion and vowed to follow the way of life of a particular religious community.
See also **bhikkhu, convent, monastery, monk, Sangha**.

Mother Theresa (1910-97) was a nun who became famous for her charity work.

This painting from 1846 shows the animals going two by two into Noah's ark.

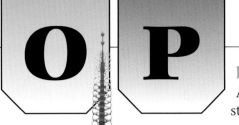

O P

observant

To be observant means to practise or follow a particular religion.

offerings

Offerings are gifts made as part of **worship** in many religions. Often the offerings are shared within the community or with others in society. See also **Buddhism**, **charity**, **Hinduism**, **murti**, **Sikhism**.

Old Testament

The Old Testament is part of the **Christian Bible**. It is made up of 39 books and is largely the same as the **Jewish scriptures** called the **Tenakh**.

ordination

Ordination is a **ceremony** at which a person officially becomes a **minister**, **priest**, **rabbi**, **monk** or **nun**. We say the person is 'ordained'.

orthodox

Orthodox means 'correct' or 'proper'. It often describes people who follow their religion very strictly.

Orthodox Church

The Orthodox Church is one of four main groups within the **Christian Church**. It developed after the Christian Church split into Eastern and Western parts in the 11th century CE. The Orthodox Church is the Eastern part and is subdivided into Eastern Orthodox (including, for example, the Greek Orthodox Church) and Oriental Orthodox (including, for example, the Orthodox Church of India).

Orthodox Christians use **candles** in their **worship** and their **churches** are often ornate. See also **Mary**, **Pentecostal Christians**, **Protestant**, **Roman Catholic**.

pagoda

A pagoda is a Japanese or Chinese style of **stupa**, a **Buddhist shrine**.

A pagoda's many layers stand for steps on the path to enlightenment.

Pali

Pali is an ancient Indian language in which the teachings of **Theravada Buddhism** were first written down.

Palm Sunday

See **Holy Week**.

Panj Piarey

Panj Piarey ('Five Beloved Ones') was the name given by **Guru Gobind Singh** to five **Sikhs** who showed themselves ready to die for their religion and became the first five members of the Sikh community, the **Khalsa**. Five Sikhs representing the Panj Piarey often lead processions at Sikh **festivals**.

parable

A parable is a 'comparing story'. It seems to be telling a simple, straightforward story but it has a more complicated message underneath. Parables are told in many religions and are used to help people understand difficult ideas or experiences.

paradise

Paradise is a name sometimes used for **heaven**. The **Qur'an** describes Paradise as a beautiful garden, full of sweet-smelling flowers, trees and gushing fountains. See also **afterlife**, **Day of Judgement**.

parochet

In a **synagogue**, the parochet is a curtain which hangs in front of the **ark**.

Passover

Passover is the English name for **Pesach**.

patriarch

A patriarch is a male head of a **family**. In the history of the **Jewish** people, **Abraham**, Isaac, Jacob and Jacob's 12 sons are patriarchs.

'Patriarch' is also used as a title for some leaders in the **Orthodox Church**.
See also **Judaism**, **matriarch**.

penance

A penance is something a person does as a punishment and to show that he or she is sorry for a wrong deed. **Roman Catholics** and **Orthodox Christians** confess (tell) their **sins** to a **priest**, who sets a penance for them to do. This might be saying some **prayers**, **fasting**, or doing a good deed. Doing the penance is believed to earn the person **God**'s **forgiveness**.

Pentecost

Pentecost is the English name for the **Jewish festival** of **Shavuot**.

There is also a different, **Christian** festival called Pentecost, seven weeks after **Easter**. It remembers the story of the **Holy Spirit** being given to **Jesus**'s **disciples**, so that they could spread the message of **Christianity**. The story is that, during the Jewish festival of Pentecost, a wind blew through the house where the disciples were and flames rested on their heads. When the disciples spoke, people of all nationalities could understand them.

Pentecostal Christians

Pentecostal Christians believe that what happened to the **disciples** at **Pentecost** still happens: that is, the **Holy Spirit** can cause people to speak words that come from **God**. Pentecostal Christianity is one of the four main groups in the **Christian Church**.
See also **Orthodox Church**, **Protestant**, **Roman Catholic**.

Pesach

Pesach is a **Jewish festival** in March or April. It remembers the **Exodus** (escape) of the ancient **Jews** from Egypt. When they left, they had no time to let their bread-dough rise before baking it, so the bread turned out flat. As a reminder of this, only unleavened (flat) bread (matzah) is eaten in the week of Pesach.

At the start of Pesach, a **service** called the Seder is held at supper time in Jewish homes. Jews read and sing from a 'haggadah', a book which tells the story of the Exodus.
See also **Judaism**.

At Pesach, some foods at the Seder are symbols reminding Jewish people of events in their history.

pilgrim, pilgrimage

A pilgrim is someone who makes a journey (called a pilgrimage) to a **holy** place or a place that is important in his or her religion. See also **Hajj**, **shrine**.

Pope

The Pope is the head of the **Roman Catholic Church**. The word Pope means 'father'. Roman Catholics believe that the Pope takes the place of **Jesus's disciple** Peter, who led the first **Christians** and was the first **bishop** of Rome. See also **Vatican City**.

Pope John Paul II was elected Pope in 1978. He became known as the 'travelling Pope', visiting countries around the world.

Poya

For **Buddhists**, Poya days (which fall on full-moon days) are days for making a special effort to go to the **vihara** and to **meditate**. They believe that all the important events in the **Buddha**'s life took place on full-moon days.

A colourful flag is put up on Poya days at this Buddhist shrine in Colombo, Sri Lanka.

prayer

Prayer means talking to **God** or to the **gods** (depending on the religion of the person who is praying).

Religious **services** usually include prayers, often with set words that are said or sung by everyone together. Also at home, or wherever they may be, people may say (or think) set prayers and prayers of their own. See also **ardas**, **Hinduism**, **Islam**, **Judaism**, **jumu'ah**, **Lord's Prayer**, **salah**.

priest

Priest is the word used for a **minister** in **Anglican**, **Orthodox Christian** and **Roman Catholic churches**. The word priest is also used for the person who leads **Hindu worship** ('puja') in a **mandir**. The Indian name for this person is a 'pujari'.

A priest is believed to be a representative of **God** or the **gods**, or to have **holy** powers. A priest is usually able to perform certain **ceremonies** that may not be performed by ordinary people. See also **Brahmin**, **ordination**.

Progressive

Progressive means 'moving forward'. Progressive **Jews** are those who believe that **Judaism** should adapt to modern times and should always be trying to move forward and improve.

prophet

In the **scriptures** of **Christianity**, **Islam** and **Judaism**, a prophet is someone who was chosen by **God** to speak to people about His wishes for the world. See also **Islam**, **Muhammad**.

Protestant

A Protestant is a type of **Christian**.
'Protest' can mean 'witness to the truth', and Protestants witness to the truth of the **Bible**. In the 16th century, some **Roman Catholics** thought their **church** had drifted away from the truths in the Bible. They wanted to change the Roman Catholic Church, but could not do so. So they formed the Protestant Church. It is now one of the four main Christian churches and includes several groups or 'denominations' such as Baptists and Methodists.

psalm

For **Christians** and **Jews**, a psalm is a song of praise to **God**. The **Bible** and the **Tenakh** include a Book of Psalms.
See also **hymn**.

puja

Puja is **worship** in **Buddhism** and **Hinduism**.

pulpit

In a **church**, a pulpit is a raised structure from which the **minister** preaches the **sermon**.

Pure Land

Pure Land is a type of **Buddhism** that developed in China and Japan. Its followers believe that a **bodhisattva** called Amitabha rules over a beautiful, peaceful world called the Pure Land. They believe that by living good lives and **worshipping** Amitabha, they will go to the Pure Land when they die and so move closer to **Nirvana**.

Purim

Purim is a **Jewish festival** in February or March. It celebrates the story of Ester, the Jewish wife of a Persian king, who saved the **Jews** from being killed by a tyrant called Haman. The story is read out at the festival and each time Haman's name appears, everyone makes a noise to try to drown it out.

Qur'an

The Qur'an is the **Islamic holy book**. **Muslims** believe that the words of the Qur'an are the words of **Allah**, giving His final guidance on how to live. They treat the book with great respect and care.

The Qur'an is divided into 114 chapters called 'surahs'. Muslims recite the first one, called 'Al-Fatihah', as part of their five daily **prayers**, and it is usually the first part of the Qur'an that Muslim children learn.
See also **Arabic, Bismillah, Gabriel, Hadith, hafiz, Islam, madrasah, Muhammad, Night of Power, salah**.

rabbi

A rabbi is a **Jewish** religious teacher who may lead **worship** in a **synagogue**. Rabbis also help and advise **Jews** in their community. **Orthodox** Jews only allow men to become rabbis. **Progressive** Jews allow both men and women to become rabbis.
See also **ordination**.

rak'ah

For **Muslims**, a rak'ah is a set of movements that must be made as they pray.
See also **Islam**.

These drawings show just four of the positions that make up a rak'ah for a Muslim woman.

Raksha Bandhan

Raksha Bandhan is a **Hindu festival** in July or August. A girl ties a bracelet made of silk or cotton around her brother's right wrist – a **symbol** of protection from **evil**. In return, he promises to look after her in the coming year. The festival comes from a story about the **god** Indra. His wife tied a lucky bracelet around his wrist which saved him from a **demon**.

Rama

Rama is a much-loved **Hindu god**, **worshipped** all over India for his goodness and courage. He and his wife Sita are the heroes of the **Ramayana**. See also **Dassehra**, **Diwali**, **Hanuman**.

At Raksha Bandhan, a girl gives her brother a lucky bracelet.

Ramadan

Ramadan is the name of a month on the **Islamic calendar**. Each Ramadan, **Muslims fast** from dawn until sunset every day. This fasting, called 'sawm', is one of the 'Five Pillars' of **Islam**. Some Muslims, including the elderly, the ill, and young children, do not have to fast.
See also **Id ul-Fitr**, **Night of Power**.

The Ramayana tells how Rama married the king's daughter, Sita, after winning an archery contest. This 18th-century painting depicts 'The Marriage of Rama and his Brothers'.

Ramayana

Part of the **Hindu scriptures**, the Ramayana is a long poem about **Rama** and his wife Sita. Sita is kidnapped by Ravana, a **demon** king, who thinks he will become ruler of the world if he marries Sita. But, with the help of **Hanuman**, Rama rescues Sita. They return home and are crowned king and queen.
See also **Dassehra**, **Diwali**.

reincarnation

Reincarnation means being born again. **Buddhists**, **Hindus** and **Sikhs** believe that, after they die, they are reborn; and that their actions in the present will affect their next life. See also **afterlife**, **karma**.

resurrection

Resurrection means coming back to life from being dead. **Christians** believe that **Jesus** rose from the dead to live forever with **God**. They hope that they too may be resurrected one day. See also **afterlife**, **Christianity**, **Easter**.

revelation

A revelation is an experience in which an important truth is revealed or made clear.

S

rite

A rite is another word for a **ceremony**. Rites of passage are ceremonies to mark a change from one stage of life to another: for example, naming, coming of age and marriage ceremonies.

ritual

A ritual is a set action performed as part of a **ceremony** or **service**.

Roman Catholic

A Roman Catholic is a **Christian** who belongs to the Roman Catholic Church, one of four main groups in the **Christian Church**. About half of all Christians are Roman Catholics. Their leader is the **Pope**.

The Roman Catholic Church developed when the Christian Church split into Eastern and Western parts in the 11th century **CE**. The Western part became the Roman Catholic Church, which has spread throughout the world.
See also **Mary**, **Orthodox Church**.

Rosh Hashanah

Rosh Hashanah is **Jewish** New Year, which falls in September or October. The **festival** celebrates how **God** created and judges the world. It is a time for thinking about the past and about how to be better in the coming year. It is the start of 'Ten Days of Repentance' (being sorry for one's sins). The **shofar** is blown at **services**, partly to 'wake up' **Jews** to repentance. See also **Yom Kippur**.

rumala

A rumala is a beautiful cloth with which **Sikhs** cover the **Guru Granth Sahib**.

Sabbath

For **Christians** and **Jews**, the Sabbath is a **holy** day of rest and **worship** each week. The idea of rest comes from the **Creation** story: **God** rested after six days of creation.

One of the **Ten Commandments** or **Sayings** is to honour and observe the Sabbath. Jews call the Sabbath **Shabbat**. It begins at sunset on Friday and lasts 25 hours. Christians have made Sunday their Sabbath because it was on a Sunday that **Jesus** rose from the dead.

sacred

Sacred is another word for **holy**.

Blowing the shofar (a ram's horn) is part of the Jewish festivals of Rosh Hashanah and Yom Kippur.

sacred thread ceremony

The sacred thread **ceremony** is a **Hindu rite** for when a boy becomes adult. It is only for the top three **castes**, and takes place traditionally when a boy is about 10. At the ceremony, a long loop of cotton is hung over the boy's left shoulder and under his right arm. He promises to read the **scriptures** and to do his duty as a Hindu. He will wear the thread for the rest of his life. See also **dharma**, **samskara**.

sacrifice

A sacrifice is a gift that a **worshipper** makes to **God** or the **gods**, at personal cost. Often the sacrifice is something the worshipper has made, grown or raised, such as an animal. People make sacrifices to say thank you, or to ask for **forgiveness** or for a **blessing**.

sadhu

A sadhu is a **Hindu holy man**. Sadhus give up their homes and belongings to spend their lives **praying** and **meditating**. They wander from place to place relying on people to give them food and money and giving their **blessing** in return.

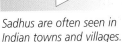

Sadhus are often seen in Indian towns and villages.

saint

For **Christians**, a saint is someone who has led an especially **holy** life and perhaps suffered for his or her religion. The **Roman Catholic Church** has officially declared people to be saints, after their death. Some Christians celebrate Saints' Days. Some saints are linked with places or activities. For example, Saint Christopher is the patron saint of travellers.
See also **halo**.

Saint Francis of Assisi called animals and birds his 'brothers and sisters'.

sajjadah

A sajjadah is a **prayer** mat used by **Muslims** to be sure that the place where they pray is clean.

salah

For **Muslims**, salah means praying five times each day. See also **Islam, Ka'aba, Night Journey, rak'ah, sajjadah, wudhu.**

samsara

In **Buddhism** and **Hinduism**, samsara is the cycle of birth, death and rebirth.

samskara

For **Hindus**, a samskara is one of 16 **ceremonies** which mark important times in their lives. For example, the 10th samskara is the **sacred thread ceremony** and the 12th samskara is a wedding.

Sangha

The Sangha is the **Buddhist** community, which began with the first people who followed the **Buddha**'s teaching. For some Buddhists, the Sangha means especially **monks** and **nuns**. For others, it includes everyone who follows the Buddha.
See also **Buddhism**.

Sanskrit

Sanskrit is an ancient Indian language in which most of the **Hindu scriptures** are written. For Hindus it is a **sacred** language.

Satan

In **Christian** and **Islamic belief**, Satan is **God**'s arch enemy who causes **evil** and **sin**. He is also called the **Devil**.

sawm

For **Muslims**, sawm is **fasting** in the month of **Ramadan**.
See also **Islam**.

scriptures

Scriptures ('writings') are **holy** books. The **Tripitaka** is one of the main **Buddhist** scriptures. The **Christian** holy book is the **Bible**. **Hindu** scriptures include the **Mahabharata**, the **Ramayana**, the **Upanishads** and the **Vedas**. The **Islamic** holy book is the **Qur'an**. The **Jewish** scriptures are called the **Tenakh**. The **Sikh** holy book is the **Guru Granth Sahib**.

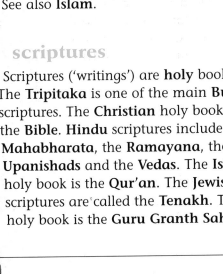

sect

A sect is a group within a religion which develops differently from the main body and sometimes splits away from it.
See also **cult**.

secular

Secular means to do with worldly matters and not with religion. A secular **Jew** is Jewish by birth but does not practise the Jewish religion.

Seder

See **Pesach**.

Sefer Torah

For **Jews**, a Sefer Torah (meaning 'Book of the Torah') is a scroll on which the words of the **Torah** are written.
See also **ark**, **etz hayim**, **Tenakh**, **yad**.

sermon

A sermon is a talk given during a **ceremony** or **service**. Sermons are important parts of some **Christian**, **Jewish** and **Muslim** services.
See also **Imam**, **khutbah**, **minbar**, **pulpit**.

Sermon on the Mount

The Sermon on the Mount is the title given in the **Gospel** of St Matthew to a collection of **Jesus**'s teachings. The Sermon includes teachings about how to treat others (for example, to love one's enemies) and about how to pray.
See also **Christianity**, **Lord's Prayer**.

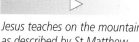

Jesus teaches on the mountain, as described by St Matthew.

service

A service is a **ceremony** or an act of **worship**. Many services follow a set pattern including **hymns**, **prayers** and readings from **scripture**.

Shabbat

For **Jews**, Shabbat is the **Hebrew** name for the seventh day of the week, which they keep as a **holy** day. It begins at sunset on Friday. In Jewish homes, two Shabbat **candles** are lit and the family sings a **prayer** called the 'kiddush', before supper. On Saturday morning many Jews go to **synagogue**. Shabbat ends just after sunset on Saturday.
See also **challah**, **Judaism**, **Sabbath**.

Shahadah

See **Islam**.

Shari'ah

For **Muslims**, the Shari'ah is a code of behaviour or law based on the **Qur'an** and the **Sunnah**.

Shavuot

Shavuot is a **Jewish festival** remembering the story of **God** giving the **Torah** to **Moses**. Shavuot also celebrates the early harvest, so Jews mark the festival by decorating **synagogues** with fruit and flowers.
See also **Judaism**, **Pentecost**.

Shema

The Shema is a **Jewish prayer**.
See also **Judaism**, **mezuzah**.

Shi'a

Shi'a is short for 'Shi'at Ali', meaning followers of Ali, the son-in-law of the **Prophet Muhammad**. Shi'a **Muslims** are Muslims who believe that true leaders of **Islam** are descended from Ali. They are guided by the teachings of their **Imams**.
See also **Sunni**.

Shinto

Shinto is an ancient religion from Japan. Its followers **worship spirits**, called kami, which include the sun **goddess** Amaterasu-o-Mikami. Her sun symbol is on the Japanese flag.

shiva

For **Jews**, shiva means seven days of mourning after a person has died.

Shiva

Shiva is one of the three main **Hindu gods**. He is the destroyer of **evil**. He is often shown holding a three-pronged fork, or trident – a **symbol** of destruction. On his forehead is an extra, all-seeing eye. Water flows through his hair. A story tells that Shiva caught the River **Ganges** in his hair as it fell from **heaven** to earth. Then he let it trickle gently across the land. Otherwise, the earth would have cracked under the river's weight.
Shiva's wife is the **goddess** Parvati.
See also **Brahma**, **Ganesha**, **Varanasi**, **Vishnu**.

Colourful posters of Shiva are often sold at temples and shrines in India.

shofar

Blown at the **Jewish festival** of **Rosh Hashanah** and at the end of **Yom Kippur**, a shofar is a ram's horn which makes a long, trumpet-like sound.

A Shinto shrine in Japan, where people worship the kami.

shrine

A shrine is a place considered **holy** because it is linked with a religious leader, **saint** or **deity**. It is often a place of **pilgrimage** and **worship**, with objects or images connected with the person or deity.

Shrove Tuesday

For **Christians**, Shrove Tuesday is the day before **Lent**. People make pancakes, traditionally to use up all the fats in the house before the Lent **fast**.

Siddhartha Gautama

Siddhartha Gautama was an Indian prince who became the **Buddha**.

Sikh

Sikh means to do with **Sikhism**. A Sikh is someone who follows Sikhism.

Sikhism

Sikhism began in Punjab, in north-west India. The religion was started in 1499 by **Guru Nanak**, and he was followed by nine more Sikh **Gurus**.

During the time of the Gurus most people in India were **Hindus**, but the country was ruled by the Mughals, who were **Muslims**. The Mughals wanted to make everyone in India become Muslim. Guru Nanak, who had been brought up as a Hindu, had a **revelation** in which he saw that all people are the children of the same one **God**. This led him to start Sikhism, a new religion of tolerance (acceptance of all religions).

Today, there are about 14 million Sikhs. Most live in India, but there are also Sikhs in other countries, especially Britain and North America.

Sikh men and wo[men] wear the five Ks a[s a] sign of their ident[ity]

The Five Ks

Sikhs wear five things to show that they are Sikhs. These are known as the Five Ks:

- *Kes*: uncut hair. This follows the example of the Gurus who did not shave or cut their hair. Men usually wear a **turban** to keep their hair tidy.
- *Kanga*: a wooden comb to keep the hair neat. It is also a **symbol** of cleanliness.
- *Kirpan*: a small sword. It is a symbol reminding Sikhs of their responsibility to defend the weak.
- *Kara*: a steel bangle. Its circle shape reminds Sikhs that God has no beginning or end. The steel reminds Sikhs to be strong.
- *Kacch*: white under-shorts, as first worn by Sikhs because they were practical for fighting; also a symbol of purity.

This is traditional Sikh costume. Most Sikh men wear Western clothes.

The Ten Sikh Gurus

❶ Guru Nanak (Guru from 1499 to 1539) made four long journeys, taking his message throughout India and beyond:

There is only one God. Worship only him. Remember God. Work hard and help others. Everyone is equal in God's eyes. It is your actions which make you good or bad. Different religions all lead to the same God. Love everyone and pray for the good of all. Always speak the truth.

❷ Guru Angad Dev (1539-52) improved the **Gurmukhi** script for writing Punjabi, the language used for all Sikh **scriptures**.
❸ Guru Amar Das (1552-74) sent out 22 Sikhs as **missionaries**, to spread Guru Nanak's teachings.
❹ Guru Ram Das (1574-81) began building the city of **Amritsar**, a religious and trading centre.
❺ Guru Arjan Dev (1581-1606) built the **Golden Temple** and collected the **Adi Granth** (scriptures). He was killed for refusing to become a Muslim.

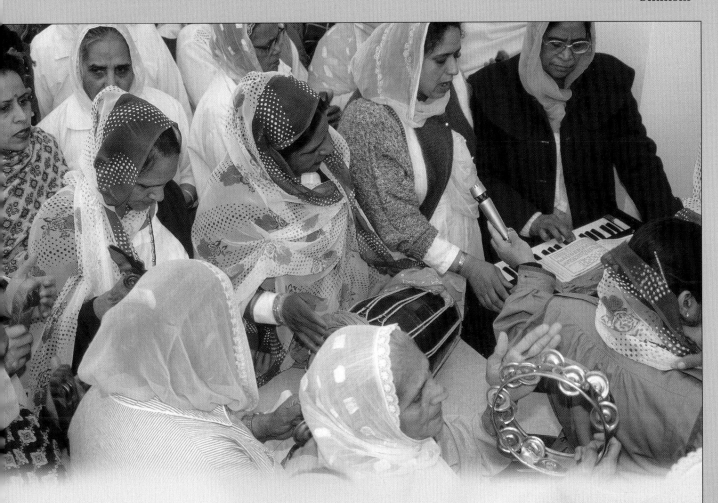

❻ Guru Hargobind (1606-44) led the Sikh fight against the Mughals.

❼ Guru Har Rai (1644-61) helped spread the Sikh religion through northern India and opened hospitals giving free medical care.

❽ Guru Har Krishan (1661-64) continued to give free medical aid. He died just eight years old.

❾ Guru Tegh Bahadur (1664-75) was killed by the Mughal emperor for refusing to give up his beliefs.

❿ **Guru Gobind Singh** (1675-1708) began the **Khalsa** (the Sikh community). He did not name a person to be Guru after him. He told the Sikhs that they must now follow the teachings of their holy book, which was named the **Guru Granth Sahib**.
He also told Sikhs to wear the Five Ks.

△

Sikh women at worship. Many Sikh women wear Punjabi suits, consisting of a dress ('kameez'), trousers ('salwar') and scarf ('dupatta').

▷

A Sikh reads from the Guru Granth Sahib. The open book is always rested on the Manji Sahib – a set of cushions and a quilt.

Going to the gurdwara

To go in to the **worship** room of their **gurdwara**, Sikhs take off their shoes and cover their heads out of respect. They bow in front of the Guru Granth Sahib, and leave **offerings** of food and money in front of it. Then they sit cross-legged on the floor. After the **service**, which includes **prayers**, **hymns** and readings from the Guru Granth Sahib, everyone shares a meal called **langar**.

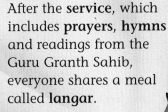
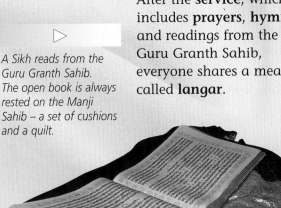

sin

For people of many religions, a sin is a thought or action which goes against what **God** commands or wishes. In **prayers**, people ask for God's **forgiveness** for their sins. See also **evil, devil, penance, Rosh Hashanah, Satan, Yom Kippur**.

Singh

Singh (meaning 'lion') is a **name** used by all **Sikh** males since the Sikh community, the **Khalsa**, was founded in 1699. For example, a Sikh boy might be called Harinder Singh. **Guru Gobind Singh** gave the names Singh to men and **Kaur** ('princess') to women, as a sign that all Sikhs are equal. The names also encouraged Sikhs to be brave in standing up for their religion.

soul

Soul is a word used by many people for the thinking, feeling part of a person, that is extra to the physical body. In many religions, the soul is believed to live on after a person dies. See also **afterlife, Day of Judgement, heaven, hell, Hinduism, paradise, reincarnation**.

spirit

Spirit is another name for a person's **soul**. It is also a name for the power which, some people believe, links everything in the universe together, including individual souls.

In some religions, for example **Shinto**, spirits are powerful, invisible beings which live inside animals, plants and natural places, such as rivers and mountains.

spiritual

Spiritual means to do with the **spirit** or **soul**. It is often used as another word for 'religious'.

A spiritual is also a type of religious song developed in America by **Christians** who were or had been slaves from Africa.

△

Prayer flags decorate the Bodnath stupa, Kathmandu, Nepal. The different parts of stupas, from the base upwards, are sometimes said to represent stages on the way to enlightenment.

stupa

A stupa is a **Buddhist shrine**. When the **Buddha** died, his remains were divided into eight and the first eight stupas were built over them, in India. Later, the remains were divided again and taken to other places where more stupas were built. Today, there are stupas all over the world. Some contain remains of the Buddha or of a Buddhist teacher or **monk**. Most contain copies of the Buddhist **scriptures**. The first stupas were dome-shaped, but other shapes have been developed. **Pagodas** are one example.

When Buddhists visit a stupa, they walk round it, clockwise, three times. This reminds them of the Three Jewels of **Buddhism**.

Sufi

Sufis are **Muslims** who use special ways, including music and dancing, to help them feel closer to **Allah**. One group of Sufis are the whirling dervishes from Turkey. They perform spectacular dances, spinning faster and faster.

'Whirling dervishes' are one type of Sufi Muslim.

Sukkot

For **Jews**, Sukkot is an autumn harvest **festival** lasting a week. The festival also remembers how the ancient Jews built shelters to live in while they were in the desert after their escape from slavery in Egypt. Today, for the festival week, Jews build and live in temporary shelters outdoors, either at home or at their **synagogue**. They must make the roofs of the shelters from materials that were, but are no longer growing; and they must be able to see the sky through the roof.
See also **Exodus**, **Judaism**.

Sunnah

The Sunnah is everything known about the **Prophet Muhammad**'s sayings, teachings, thoughts and actions. It is made up of the **Hadith** and the 'Sirah' (the story of the Prophet's life). **Sunni Muslims** use the Sunnah as a guide in their lives and to help them understand the **Qur'an**.
See also **Shari'ah**.

Sunni

Sunni is the name for **Muslims** who are guided by the **Sunnah** in their daily lives. About four-fifths of Muslims today are Sunni.
See also **Shi'a**.

sutra

Sutra is a **Sanskrit** word meaning 'thread'. It is used to describe a verse or longer piece of writing in the **Buddhist** or **Hindu** **scriptures**. Each sutra is a 'thread' of thought about a topic. Buddhists often write sutra as 'sutta'.

symbol

A symbol is a sign, picture, object or action that stands for something more than it looks.

synagogue

A synagogue is a place where **Jews** go to **worship**, attend classes about their religion, and meet for social events.

Many Jews go to synagogue on **Shabbat** and at **festivals**. Some synagogues have **services** every day. In some synagogues, men and women sit apart. In others, everyone sits together.
See also **ark**, **bimah**, **Judaism**, **parochet**, **Ner Tamid**, **rabbi**, **Ten Sayings**.

Palm, willow, myrtle and citron are four plants used as symbols at the Sukkot festival.

takht

In a **gurdwara**, a takht is a kind of throne, a platform with a canopy, on which the **Guru Granth Sahib** is placed.
See also **chauri, Manji Sahib, rumala**.

Talmud

The Talmud is a collection of **Jewish** writings dating from about 200 to 500 **CE**. The writings record the thoughts of many early **rabbis** (Jewish teachers) who studied and discussed the meaning of the **Torah**.

Taoism

Taoism is an ancient religion followed today by about 5 million people in China, Japan and other parts of South East Asia. It was begun by Lao-tzu, a Chinese philosopher, in the 6th century **BCE**. He taught people about a great power in the world called the Tao, or 'the Way'. Taoists try to live good lives so that they can become part of the Tao.

temple

In several religions, the word temple is sometimes used for a place of **worship**.

For **Jews**, Temple (with a capital T) means their ancient Temple in **Jerusalem**. It was built in the time of King Solomon, 3,000 years ago. Conquerors from Babylon destroyed the building in 586 **BCE**, but the Jews won back Jerusalem and rebuilt the Temple. It was destroyed again by the Romans in 70 **CE**. Only one wall – the **Western Wall** – was left standing. Jews today travel from all over the world to pray at the Western Wall.
See also **Hanukah, Judaism, menorah**.

It is thought that Lao-tzu, the founder of Taoism, is the figure on the right in this 14th-century painting.

Confucianism and Taoism include ancient Chinese ideas, such as that the world is made up of opposing forces, yin and yang, which balance each other. This is the symbol of yin and yang.

temptation

Temptation (or tempting someone) means trying to make someone do what he or she feels is wrong.
See also **Lent**.

Ten Commandments

The Ten Commandments are ten laws which **Christians** and **Jews** use as their main guide for how **God** wants them to behave. They believe that God gave the laws to **Moses** on Mount Sinai.

The Ten Commandments are found in the book of **Exodus** in the **Old Testament** and in the **Torah**.

The first Commandments say how people should **worship** and respect God. The rest set out how people should behave towards each other. They include 'Honour your father and your mother', 'Do not commit murder', 'Do not steal' and 'Do not tell lies'.
See also **Ten Sayings**.

Ten Sayings

The Ten Sayings is a name used by **Jews** for the **Ten Commandments**. The Sayings are displayed on the wall in most **synagogues**. Sometimes they are made to look as if they are written on two stone tablets – like the tablets on which **Moses** received the Sayings, according to the **Torah**.

Tenakh

The Tenakh is the name of the **Jewish scriptures**. It is divided into three parts: the **Torah** (5 Books of Teaching); the **Nevi'im** (21 Books of the **Prophets**); and the Ketuvim (13 Books of Writings). The initials of the parts – T, N and K – lead to the word Tenakh. The Tenakh is also called the **Hebrew**, or Jewish, **Bible**. See also **Old Testament**.

Theravada Buddhism

Theravada Buddhism is one of two main types of **Buddhism**. It is older than the other type, called **Mahayana**. Theravada **Buddhists** believe that the only way to reach **enlightenment** is by following the teachings of the **Buddha**.

In Theravada Buddhism, there is a particular relationship between the **Sangha** (**monks** and **nuns**) and 'lay' (ordinary) Buddhists. The monks and nuns rely on lay Buddhists to give them food and other things they need. In return, by their good example, the monks and nuns help and guide the lay community. See also **Pali**, **Tripitaka**.

A Torah scroll may be kept in a wooden or metal case.

Torah

For **Jews**, the Torah ('teaching') is the most important part of their **scriptures** (see **Tenakh**). The five books in the Torah include stories about the first Jews and more than 600 laws (**mitzvot**). Every **Shabbat**, a passage from the Torah is read out in the **synagogue**. Over a year, the whole Torah is read. It is always read in **Hebrew**.
See also **ark**, **Sefer Torah**, **Talmud**.

Tripitaka

The Tripitaka is the **Theravada Buddhist scriptures**. The name means 'Three Baskets' – probably because the scriptures were first written on palm leaves which were stored in baskets. The first basket, or part, contains rules for **monks**. The second has the **Buddha**'s teachings and stories about his life. The third has more teachings.
See also **Dhammapada**.

turban

A turban is a long piece of cloth which a **Sikh** man winds around his head to keep his long hair tidy. Sikh boys wear simpler head coverings called 'patka' and 'rumal'.
See also **Sikhism**.

This Sikh is wearing a khanda-symbol pin in his turban.

U V

Ummah

See **Islam**.

Upanishads

The Upanishads are **Hindu scriptures** dating from about 2,500 years ago. They take the form of lessons given by **gurus** to their pupils, and they talk about the relationship between people and Brahman (see **Hinduism**). Many stories are used to explain difficult points. At first, the Upanishads were remembered and passed on by word of mouth. Later they were written down in **Sanskrit**. There are more than 100 Upanishads.

Varanasi

Varanasi (also known as Benares) is a city on the banks of the River **Ganges** in northern India. For **Hindus** it is a **holy** place, visited by millions of **pilgrims** every year. They bathe in the river, which they believe is **sacred**. They also visit some of the hundreds of **temples** in the city. Most of these are dedicated to the **god Shiva**. A story says that Shiva chose Varanasi as his home on earth. He also placed it at the centre of the earth to show its great holiness and importance.

Vatican City

The Vatican City is a tiny country inside the city of Rome in Italy. It is the centre of the **Roman Catholic Church** and the home of its leader, the **Pope**.

Hindus bathe in the River Ganges, at Varanasi and at other sacred places.

▷

Crowds go to the Vatican for Mass led by the Pope.

Vedas

The Vedas are some of the oldest **Hindu scriptures**, dating from about 3,500 years ago. There are four Vedas. The first is the Rig Veda, which means the 'Song of Knowledge'. It contains over 1,000 **hymns** in praise of the **gods** and **goddesses**. For many hundreds of years the Vedas were memorized and passed on by word of mouth. Eventually they were written down in **Sanskrit**.

vicar

Vicar is the name used for the **minister** in some **Christian churches**. It means 'representative' of God.

New Delhi

Varanasi [Benares]

Calcutta

I N D I A

Bombay

Arabian Sea

Bay of Bengal

Madras

vihara

A vihara is a place where **Buddhist monks** and **nuns** live. When **Buddhism** began, in India, the rainy season stopped the monks from travelling about to teach. They built huts to shelter in and these were the first viharas. Viharas now have living quarters for the monks and nuns, meeting and **meditation** rooms, a library, and a **shrine** room with a statue of the **Buddha**. Some viharas also have a **stupa**.

As well as being the place where monks and nuns live, the vihara is where ordinary Buddhists go to **worship** and to celebrate **festivals**. The vihara is sometimes called a **monastery** and sometimes called a **temple**.

Vishnu

Vishnu is one of the three main **Hindu gods**. He is the protector of the world and the god of goodness and mercy. He is often shown with four hands, holding a conch shell, a **lotus** flower and two weapons, a discus and a club. Hindus believe that Vishnu visits the earth from time to time, to save the world from danger. His wife is Lakshmi, the **goddess** of beauty and wealth. See also **Brahma**, **Hinduism**, **Shiva**.

vow

A vow is a solemn promise made to **God** or the **gods**, or to a marriage partner.

water

Water appears in the **scriptures** and **rituals** of several religions, as a **symbol** of refreshment, purity or new birth.

See also **baptism**, **Ganges**, **wudhu**, **Zamzam**.

Many Jews go to pray at the Western Wall. Some put their prayers on paper into cracks in the wall.

Wesak

For **Theravada Buddhists**, Wesak is a **festival** in May which marks the birth, **enlightenment** and death of the **Buddha**. Buddhists send Wesak cards and decorate their homes and **viharas** with lanterns and flowers. On Wesak day they try to be especially kind and generous.

Western Wall

The Western Wall is the only remaining part of the ancient **Jewish Temple** in **Jerusalem**.

worship

To worship can mean to respect and adore. It can also mean to express respect and adoration, perhaps by taking part in a religious **service**.

wudhu

For **Muslims**, wudhu is a **ritual** of washing before they pray. They wash their face, hands, arms and feet three times each in water and then wipe their hair with their damp hands or palms. **Mosques** have special areas for wudhu. See also **Islam**.

Y Z

yad

A yad (meaning 'hand') is a pointer used by **Jews** to keep the place when reading from a **Sefer Torah**. The end of a yad is often shaped like a hand.

yoga

Yoga is a technique practised by some **Hindus** who believe that it can help them to break free from the cycle of birth, death and rebirth (**samsara**). The technique involves exercises, controlled breathing and **meditation**. Some people practise yoga to help them feel calmer and healthier. See also **Hinduism**.

Yom Kippur

For **Jews**, Yom Kippur is the last of the 'Ten Days of Repentance' which begin at **Rosh Hashanah**. On Yom Kippur, many Jews go to **synagogue** to pray for **forgiveness** for their wrongs over the past year. Yom Kippur is also a day of **fasting**. A **shofar** is blown to mark the end of the fast.

Zakah

See **Islam**.

Zamzam

Zamzam is the name of a well in **Makkah**. **Muslims** believe that the **angel** Jibril (**Gabriel**) showed the well to Hagar, **Ibrahim**'s wife, when she was searching for **water** for her son Isma'il. Muslims on **Hajj** in Makkah drink Zamzam water, and take some home for their friends and relations.

Zen

Zen is a type of **Buddhism** followed in Japan and China. For Zen **Buddhists**, **meditation** is the way to reach **enlightenment**. They practise many activities as forms of meditation, including poetry, painting and martial arts, such as kung fu and karate. These all require concentration and so help to focus the mind.

At a Zen monastery in Honshu, Japan, this garden of raked sand and stepping stones across moss helps the monks to meditate.

Zion, Zionism

For **Jews**, Zion has several meanings. It is the hill on which **Jerusalem** was built. The name is also used, especially in the **Tenakh** and in **Jewish prayers**, for Jerusalem itself or even for the land of **Israel**. Third, Zion can mean what is hoped for: the Jews' return to the land of Israel or a perfect life for all people.

Zionism is a name for the desire and effort of Jews to return to Israel and to strengthen Jewish **culture**. Zionism began as an active movement over 100 years ago in Europe.

Zoroastrianism

Zoroastrianism is a religion which was started by a man called Zoroaster in ancient Persia (Iran) more than 3,000 years ago. Zoroaster taught that there was one **god**, Ahura Mazda, who had made the world in order to destroy the **evil spirit** Angra Mainyu; and that life is a battle between good and bad. Zoroastrians are also called Parsis, which means 'Persian'. Today there are about 150,000 Parsis. Most of them live in India.